Online Collaborative Learning
Communities

Online Collaborative Learning Communities

*Twenty-One Designs to Building
an Online Collaborative
Learning Community*

CHIH-HSIUNG TU

LIBRARIES
UNLIMITED
A Member of the Greenwood Publishing Group

Westport, Connecticut, and London

Library of Congress Cataloging-in-Publication Data

Tu, Chih-Hsiung.

Online collaborative learning communities : twenty-one designs to building an online collaborative learning community / Chih-Hsiung Tu.

p. cm.

Includes index.

ISBN 1-59158-155-9 (pbk. : alk. paper)

1. Computer-assisted instruction.   2. Instructional systems—Design.   3. Group work in education.   4. Computer conferencing in education. I. Title.

LB1028.5.T755   2004

371.33′4—dc22   2004048924

British Library Cataloguing in Publication Data is available.

Library of Congress Catalog Card Number: 2004048924

ISBN: 1-59158-155-9

First published in 2004

Libraries Unlimited, 88 Post Road West, Westport, CT 06881

An imprint of Greenwood Publishing Group Inc.

www.librariesunlimited.com

Printed in the United States of America

The paper used in this book complies with the Permanent Paper Standard issued by the National Information Standards Organization (Z39.48-1984).

10 9 8 7 6 5 4 3 2 1

To Gayle

Human knowledge power is not what we know and what we possess; it is what we share with others about what we know.

Contents

Illustrations   *x*

Preface   *xi*

I. Background and Theory   **1**

Chapter 1   Introduction   3
   Why This Book?   5
   What Will You Learn from This Book?   6
   How to Use This Book   8
   Background   9

Chapter 2   Concepts of Online Collaborative Learning   11
   Interactivity   12
   Social Context   14
   Technologies   18
   Assessment in Collaboration   21
   Evaluations of Teaching on Online Collaborative Instructions   26
   Future Issues   28
   Reflections   28

II. Implementation   **29**

Chapter 3   Preparation   31
   Design 1 Communication and Preparation   31
   Design 2 Team Goals/Objectives Setting   34
   Reflections   38

Chapter 4   Collaboration, Interactive Assignments   39
       Design 3 Peer Support Assignment   39
       Design 4 Interactive Project Presentation   43
       Reflections   45

Chapter 5   Collaboration, Interactive Engagements   47
       Design 5 Online Moderation   47
       Design 6 Online Debate   52
       Reflections   63

Chapter 6   Beyond the Class Community   65
       Design 7 Virtual Experts   65
       Design 8 Guest Moderators   71
       Reflections   72

Chapter 7   E-CoP   73
       Design 9 Building a CoP   74
       Design 10 Electronic Media for CoP   77
       Design 11 Social Relationship for CoP   81
       Reflections   83

Chapter 8   Technology   85
       Design 12 Communication Technology   86
       Design 13 Collaboration Tools   89
       Design 14 Selecting Appropriate Online Communication 94
       Reflections   96

Chapter 9   Social Collegial   97
       Design 15 Understanding Social Context   97
       Design 16 Optimizing Online Interactivity   101
       Reflections   105

Chapter 10   Assessment   107
       Design 17 Collaborative Evaluation   107
       Design 18 Reflections   112
       Reflections   113

III. Beyond the Designs   115

Chapter 11   Collaborative Evaluation of Teaching   117
       Design 19 Preliminary Communication   118
       Design 20 Online Evaluation and Discussions   120
       Design 21 Feedback and Debriefing   123
       Reminders   123
       Reflections   124

Chapter 12   Finis   125
        Slow Social Change   125
        Appreciation of Values   126
        Accountability of Assessment   126
        Appropriate Use of Technologies   127
        Fear of Sufficient Content Coverage   127
        Reflections   127

Appendix: A Collaborative Evaluation Form   129

Resources   131
        Online Collaborative Learning   131
        Online Debate   131
        Online Moderations   132
        Community of Practice (CoP)   132

References   133

Index   139

Illustrations

Figure 3.1	Checklist for the Online Teams	37
Figure 4.1	The Guidelines on How to Review Teammates' Assignment and Provide Feedback	41
Figure 5.1	Moderation Guidelines	49
Figure 5.2	Online Debate Instructions	57
Figure 5.3	The Tasks and Guidelines for the Online Debate Moderators	59
Figure 6.1	Guidelines for Communicating with Virtual Experts	68
Figure 8.1	The Advantages and Disadvantages of File Management Systems	91
Figure 8.2	The Continuum of Relation of CMC Forms and Social Context Cues	95
Figure 8.3	The Continuum of Relation of CMC Forms and Response Time	95
Figure 10.1	The Possible Combinations of Peer and Self-Evaluation Based on a Three-Learner Team	109
Figure 10.2	Guidelines for Setting Up Team Governance	110
Figure 10.3	How to Evaluate Peer's Performance	111

Preface

Online teaching is a popular way to deliver instruction at any level of education. As an online instructor, I am always searching for effective technology-based instructional designs to improve my students' learning and my online teaching.

I remember the experiences I gained and the lessons I learned from the first time that I taught an online course. I posted all of my course materials online at the beginning of the semester, asked my students to participate in asynchronous discussions like threaded discussions and real-time discussions, and required students to conduct a few assignments. This sounded like typical online teaching of online courses. Unfortunately, I learned a hard lesson. Shortly after the class started, I found that none of the students participated in the asynchronous discussions. Afterward, the students told me that it wasn't required because there were no points assigned to the discussions so that is why they did not participate.

The following semester, the online discussion design was changed and a grade assigned. Then I learned another lesson. Students responded to my discussion questions and never returned to the discussion board to continue further online discussion. After posting, they disappeared. The online discussion activity was more completing assignments or answering questions with short answers. It was rare to see students respond to each other's postings in the discussion areas.

Another situation was that none of the students submitted postings during the week. When the weekend arrived, all the messages suddenly flooded in. As an inexperienced online instructor, I didn't want to do the course work during the weekend; I wanted my weekends to be my own with free time away from work. Unfortunately, some technical issues and irrelevant messages occurred during the weekend. Of course, I was not aware of the problems until on Monday when I looked at the discussion area. So I decided to require students to do group projects, because applying collaborative learning for face-to-face classes is an effective way to teach. I assumed it should work in online learning courses as well.

I grouped the students together and assigned them the projects. Some groups came back with the exactly what I expected while some did not. I consistently heard students complaining that their partners were not doing any work, not responding to their e-mail, or they even had fights within the group or between the groups. I ended up spending all my time putting out fires throughout the course. Before the course was half over, I was worn out. I asked myself what I did wrong. I prepared everything for my course as I would when teaching in face-to-face classrooms. I read online instructional design articles and books. But I was not clear about how I should design my online courses.

One of my fellow online instructors shared his online teaching experiences with me. One of his students didn't participate in any class activity until the last week of the course. Within one week, this student finished all of the requirements. He had to assign a grade to this student because he did not clearly specify limits for any class activities. His was another online teaching story that ended in failure.

I was hoping there was a book that would help me find a more practical way to teach online without just throwing tons of theories and concepts at me. I was looking for guidelines and guidance to help me to teach effectively online. Unfortunately, I was unable to find such a book. With more experiences and consistently piloting different online teaching strategies and instructional designs, I found integrating collaborative learning, online learning, and learning community into an online learning environment is an effective way to enhance learning. I read research in online learning, and I designed some online activities, conducted research in my classes, and improved my teaching based on my research results and my students' feedback. My colleagues feel that the activities in which I engaged students in online learning were very interesting and effective. I was encouraged to share my online class designs with others; therefore, I was motivated to gather all my course designs in online collaborative learning community and to publish it as a book to share with other educators who are confronting the same experiences I encountered as a novice online teacher.

Applying online collaborative learning community does not mean that teachers will spend less time with the class and the students. As educators, we all know that we would like students to learn effectively and become active learners rather than just deliver the information to the students. We are passionately involved in education and teaching. Regardless of how we teach, we want our students to become active learners. I hope this book will provide effective online teaching methods combine with your passion for education and online teaching to fulfill our common goals: generating knowledge through interaction; and contributing to the growth, professions, and community of learning through continual improvement of our teaching.

PART I

Background and Theory

Part I is the foundation of this book. Two chapters provide the instruction on how to use this book and covers the theoretical background of the online collaborative learning community.

CHAPTER 1

Introduction

Scenario 1:

Instructor, "Class, we are going to do a collaborative learning project over the next two weeks. I would like you to form teams of three to five people each. Your project is . . . . It is due one week from today. Only one report from each team is to be turned in."

Scenario 2:

"Assignment 3 is a collaborative assignment. Students are assigned to a group with three to four persons. Students have two weeks to finish this team project. Each team should . . . ."

How often have we seen this type of collaborative learning in face-to-face or online classrooms regardless of the scholastic level? This is what most people think of as collaborative learning and learning community. Students are asked to get together and perform team tasks. Frequently, when collaborative learning is applied to an online course, the only difference that exists is that oral conversation is conducted with written electronic texts. Is this what we call collaborative learning or online learning community? Does this form of collaboration enhance online learning?

Integrating technology into teaching and learning isn't just an issue for online learning, but also for technology-based learning and hybrid classes that mix face-to-face instruction and technology-based learning.

Integration isn't just putting technology into a class for teaching and learning or just using technology to deliver instruction, such as putting the syllabus online. Frequently, practitioners and instructional designers transfer FTF lectures directly to online teaching. Online lecturing, such as posting lecture notes online, isn't an effective way to conduct online teaching; therefore, we must provide effective instructional activities to enhance online learning rather than applying face-to-face instructional activities for online learning. Technology should bring learners together rather than isolating them, although it allows them to learn at different times and in different places. Without effective designs and activities to engage learners in active learning, they frequently feel that they work in isolation. Therefore, learners feel detached. Effective online learning strategies should engage learners in active learning; therefore, learners will feel that even though they may work alone they are learning together online. This is where the online learning community fits in.

Collaborative learning is one of the most frequently adopted instructional design strategies for online learning. Instructors and instructional designers apply this technique to enhance learning in both face-to-face classrooms and technology-based courses. Active learning and involved interaction are not maximized through brief episodes of collaboration. A single team project accomplished over an abbreviated period of time fails to generate a full-range of active learning and interaction. Furthermore, learners are denied leadership in their own learning and are degraded to a passive stance in their education. Collaborative learning is frequently misunderstood as simply doing team projects, working in teams, sharing project responsibilities, etc. This lack of understanding prevents capturing the true meaning of collaborative learning, active learning, and interaction. Simply assigning learners a team project and establishing a team for a limited period provides a less than ideal learning experience. Ideal collaboration involves learners in active team participation in multiple tasks throughout the entire learning process inside and outside of the class. A learning community is often developed through this increased interaction.

The availability of advanced computer technologies permits the use of computer-mediated communication (CMC) for forming and sustaining online learning communities. An online learning community remains one of the most popular concepts for technology-based learning in education. Teammates communicating with each other, learning together, searching for resources, supporting each other, conducting team projects online, and solving real-life problems have become important activities in the learning process. Instructors have valued the importance of the concept of the online learning community. Many of them have integrated this concept into their collaborative instruction and promote it for learning activities.

More advanced technologies should be applied to foster self-improving communities. It is important to move beyond a forum for exchanging tidbits and opinions, to structures that readily capture knowledge-value and foster rapid accumulation and growth of a community's capabilities. Therefore, a learning community will lead to the development of more personalized, self-adaptive learning systems. For example, threading of commentary found in an online threaded discussion board does not support complicated human thinking; and, it is time-consuming to read all of the threads in an active discussion. Given the opportunity learners readily find the best resources that are necessary for knowledge mining and knowledge construction and contribute it to the community.

The purpose of this book is to provide an effective and comprehensive guide for instructors, in all positions, who are interested in integrating online collaboration into their instruction. Pre-service teachers, instructional designers, and media specialists may find this book particularly useful for preparing their online instructional designs and teaching preparations. The usefulness of an online collaborative learning community is to allow learners and instructors who are working at a different time and in a different place but are able to create the community sense to support the learning and teaching. One of the most powerful characteristics of digital technologies is the ability to separate special and interval aspects (time and place) and communication channels (audio and visual). These powerful capabilities could be a double-edged sword. With appropriate use of technology, online learners and their teacher are empowered and are able to manipulate these characteristics of technology and generate stronger community sense in the learning and teaching. By contrast, the community sense could be diminished due to the isolation that results from inappropriate design and use of online technology. With pervasive online technology, teachers and media specialists/instructional designers have been asked or even required to integrate advanced technology to teach online via use of an effective online collaborative learning community. This book becomes an important guide to those who wish to integrate technology into online learning.

This book does not dwell on lofty theories but offers practical guidelines that are based on effective, current theories, solid frameworks, and the extensive online teaching experience of the author. Three major learning theories, online learning, and community learning constitute the foundation of this book on collaborative learning. It is for practitioners to use in the field, but researchers and others may also find it is useful because the strategies, guidelines, and activities discussed have resulted from many years of online teaching and are based on comprehensive research performed by the author.

WHY THIS BOOK?

Many of the books currently available about online collaboration and the online learning community are written for academics and researchers as a result of research studies or specific classroom instruction. Few books are designated for classroom teachers and corporate trainers. Classroom instructors and corporate trainers find it difficult to apply modern learning concepts to their teaching because the application of theoretical frameworks is very difficult and very time-consuming. Therefore, a comprehensive guidebook is needed to design and build an ideal online collaborative learning community (OCLC).

Another reason a comprehensive guidebook is needed is that many educators feel that simply asking learners to work together to produce a team project online will result in an ideal collaborative learning outcome. This is not necessarily true. This book provides twenty-one effective designs with guidelines, strategies, examples, and tips to assist readers in designing their own OCLC instruction regardless of grade levels or delivery systems (online, face-to-face, or mixed/blended).

This book functions as a comprehensive guide to plan, organize, build, facilitate, nurture, sustain, and assess ideal and effective OCLCs. It is written in plain language and is easy for classroom instructors and corporate trainers to understand, especially those with very limited instructional design experience and technology expertise, or those who do not want spend an enormous amount of time dealing with technology. Pre-service teachers and media specialists/instructional designers may find this particularly useful to their practices and further teaching in online environments. The individual with a limited instructional design and technology background is able to understand the concepts presented and adopt them into their instruction immediately. The readers will find that the step-by-step design renders the adoption and application of an OCLC easier. Many step-by-step instructions are accompanied with readily adopted designs, tasks, guidelines, strategies, examples, and tips to allow readers to plan a comprehensive and effective OCLC for their teaching. Readers may use the examples outlined in this book and integrate them into their OCLC, such as Peer Assignment Support Guidelines, or Moderation Guidelines, in addition to the associated step-by-step instructions.

WHAT WILL YOU LEARN FROM THIS BOOK?

The readers of this book will learn the true meaning of an OCLC and how to build an ideal OCLC for online teaching or they may use this book as a supplement to their traditional teaching. The book is divided into three main parts, Part I Background and Theory, Part II Implementation, and Part III Beyond the Design. Part I includes two chapters that discuss the background of this book and the theoretical framework of OCLC including three elements, Interactivity, Social Context, and Technology. This framework allows the readers to start building their own OCLCs with effective technology integration. Part II is the muscle of this offering and contains eight chapters that provide step-by-step instructions and strategies for building OCLCs. Part III includes two chapters that discuss the evaluations of online teaching, and summarize and identify the weaknesses of an OCLC while applying the twenty-one designs into online instruction.

Chapter 2, Concepts of Online Collaborative Learning, provides three important elements (interactivity, social context, and technologies) for building an OCLC. The purpose of this chapter is to provide a theoretical basis for collaborative learning in the online learning community with support from various technologies. This is an ideal chapter to learn what theories support OCLC and the twenty-one designs introduced in this book.

Chapter 3, Preparation, contains Design 1 (Communication and Preparation) and Design 2 (Team Goals/Objectives Setting), which discuss the practical collaborative activities to be implemented on a regular basis to sustain an OCLC through continuing collaborative activities while maintaining good communication with learners.

Chapters 4, 5, and 6 focus on the collaboration activities and include six designs (Peer Support Assignments, Interactive Project Presentation, Online Moderation, Online Debate, Virtual Experts, and Guest Moderators). These designs engage learners in online collaboration and internal and external online communities.

Chapter 7, E-CoP, is a unique chapter in this book for those in corporate training and educators who are interested in the concepts of supporting teams and learning community. Communities of practice (CoPs) are groups of people who share similar goals, interests, and practices and, in doing so, employ common practices, work with the same tools, and express themselves in a common language. This chapter provides designs to integrate electronic communication technologies to support employees, staff, and interest groups to enhance their practices.

Chapter 8, Technology, covers useful and effective online collaboration tools. These tools include communication tools, collaboration tools, and management tools.

Chapter 9, Social Collegial, suggests useful communication designs and strategies to build cohesion among online members to build social cohesion in the OCLC.

Chapter 10, Assessment, is designated for the evaluation of collaborative learning and includes Design 17, Collaborative Evaluation, and Design 18, Reflection. Although many ongoing evaluations are embodied in other online activities, the focus is given to the team project evaluation and overall OCLC learning experiences in this chapter. The second design in this chapter is designated for reflections of the student and their experiences on their OCLC. Effective strategies are introduced to assist instructors in design activities to help learners to reflect on their learning experiences and to project on how they will improve their OCLC skills for any future learning tasks.

Chapter 11, Collaborative Evaluation of Teaching, is a chapter that goes beyond the learners' online collaboration. The integration of student evaluation of teaching and peer evaluation of teaching grants instructors valuable feedback to improve their OCLC design and teaching skills. This chapter is particularly useful for administrators to assess and evaluate the instructor's performance of their online teaching.

Chapter 12, the last chapter, is a summary and recommends strategies for the post-class stage of an OCLC. This chapter outlines several weaknesses incurred when adopting the concept of an OCLC. Being aware of the weaknesses of an OCLC will fortify readers with realistic expectations and can be important in preventing failures.

The Appendix "Resources" deals with building an OCLC. The use of resources will ensure and enhance the talents of the readers and enable them to foster and sustain a healthy OCLC.

HOW TO USE THIS BOOK

This book is written for different levels of use. The readers can use this book to prepare, improve, and enhance their online teaching through empowering their learners. One may find that one chapter or one design is more useful than the others because each of us come from different areas of expertise. Reading the entire book is appropriate in order to gain a better understanding of how to build an OCLC; but certain chapters and designs may contain strategies and guidelines that are more appropriate for individual classrooms.

Instructors interested in adopting effective online collaboration instruction will find that studying Parts II and III will result in effective adaptation. It is recommended that instructional designers and specialists focusing on the development of various guidelines will provide better support in terms of instruction development, such as online debate guidelines, online moderation guidelines, and peer evaluation guidelines. These guidelines will empower learners to determine and negotiate their collaborative learning validated by learner-centered and even learner-driven concepts.

Researchers who would like to explore the theories and framework behind the OCLC may find Chapter 2, Concepts of Online Collaborative Learning, more informative. If they are interested additional theories or framework, it is recommended that they peruse the original texts of the references cited in this chapter. For administrators involved in teaching evaluation, each design provided throughout the book will provide a good idea what ideal online teaching should look like and will permit them to determine what and how to evaluate online teaching.

Each of the twenty-one designs starts with the specifics that represent key elements of each design. These specifics (What, Who, When, How, Technology, Duration, and Grade) give the readers an overview of the design.

BACKGROUND

Guidelines, instructions, and strategies provided in this book are based on current theoretical frameworks in an online learning community, recent studies, and recent publications and practices that have been successful in online classes that the author has designed and taught. The material presented is derived from lessons learned from teaching online courses and experiences gleaned in online classrooms. The author's professional career has developed through the use of technology in online communities. It is the author's belief that his experience in online teaching will provide an excellent resource for those who are interested in OCLC.

CHAPTER 2

Concepts of Online Collaborative Learning

This chapter provides a theoretical foundation for collaborative learning in the online community through multiple computer technologies. Three key concepts, collaborative learning, online learning, and community learning in addition to the assessment of teaching and learning, are the foundation of this chapter that sustain the designs introduced later in this book. The theoretical framework discussed in this chapter is composed of three major constructs (interactivity, social context, and technologies) (Tu & Corry, 2002). Interactivity concerns the concepts and designs that engage learners in active collaboration. Social context refers to the learner-centered learning community. The third construct details technologies that support and enhance knowledge development and knowledge management. These constructs form a framework and provide readers with a theoretical overview to build and sustain an interactive online collaborative learning community. These constructs are not contained within well-marked boundaries, they blend and overlap and one element cannot be implemented without the other two. Another key concept integrating collaborative learning into online learning is "community." The sense of "community" must be sustained when implementing online collaborative learning. In addition to the theoretical framework of online collaborative learning community, the assessment of collaborative learning and teaching is discussed later in this chapter.

Collaboration is distinguished from cooperation throughout this book. Many authors use these terms interchangeably, but collaborative learning may be fostered differently than cooperative learning. In general, they are called small-group instruction. This book focuses on collaboration, but many of the theoretical constructs, strategies, and guidelines can be applied to cooperation. It is necessary for readers to grasp the characteristics of both concepts. In practice, most educators apply a mixture of both strategies to their instruction.

Here are the main points distinguishing collaboration and cooperation:

Collaboration

- Applies small-group activities as strategies to develop higher-order thinking skills and enhance individual abilities to master knowledge
- Encourages the laissez-faire approach for higher-level, less-foundational knowledge content
- Assumes that knowledge is socially constructed
- Is applied in colleges

Cooperation

- Encourages an explorer approach but in a more structured manner for the foundational knowledge typified in gateway instruction
- Assumes knowledge that is socially constructed but is the methodology of choice for foundational knowledge
- Is applied in primary school

INTERACTIVITY

Interactivity includes collaboration and active learning. Collaboration does not occur unless learners are granted authority over and are actively engaged in their learning activities.

Collaboration

Collaborative learning uses small groups of learners in the instruction encouraging them to maximize their own, and each other's, learning. Collaborative learning engages learners in knowledge sharing, inspiring each other, depending upon each other, and applying active social interaction in a small group. Therefore, collaborative learning depends upon the art of social interaction among learners rather than a mechanical process. "Collaborative learning is a personal philosophy, not just a classroom technique. In all situations where people come together in groups, it suggests a way of dealing with people, which respects and highlights individual group members' abilities and contributions. There is a sharing of authority and acceptance of responsibility among group members for the group's actions" (Panitz, 1996). Instructors shift their authority, under the auspices of ideal collaborative learning, to the learners and provide the foundation and learning structures to guide them through various learning processes and experiences and through active social interaction on substantive issues by applying modern technology. "Good learning, like good work, is collaborative and social, not competitive and isolated. Sharing one's ideas and responding to others' improves thinking and deepens understanding" (Gerdy, 1998).

Merely corralling learners into groups does not assure ideal collaborative learning. Four important issues must be considered when integrating online collaboration into instruction: empowering learners, building communities, continuing support, and being patient. Regardless of how collaborative learning is implemented, these four important issues must not be neglected.

Empowering learners

Instructors must empower learners in any online learning environment (Dickstein, 1998). Learners should be accountable for their learning and determine what, how, when, and where to learn. Therefore, instructors become facilitators to guide learners through different learning processes, permitting a variety of elements to accommodate different learning styles rather than attempting to force everyone into the same learning pattern. Some structure is necessary, but care must be exercised to prevent it from becoming too rigid, for example, a step-by-step instruction. Empowering learners is a difficult task for instructors because they must risk passing authority to their learners.

Building communities

Humans learn through rich social interaction in a community (Tu & Corry, 2002). Learners must associate and connect internally in the classroom and externally with other learners and instructors. This allows the review of multiple perspectives and enriches the learning experiences (Honebein, 1996).

Continuing support

The process of collaborative learning must be constantly reinforced. The objectives of collaborative learning must be explained in detail to ensure that learners understand it clearly. Providing seamless intellectual, technical, social, mental, and emotional support throughout the entire learning process allows learners to demonstrate their independence. Frequently, learners embark upon a course of study with the simple expectation of a good grade; but they evolve into learning independently when they understand the process and have appropriate support. The absence of adequate support is a major failure. Time-consuming? Yes, it is a time-consuming process that engages learners in an enriched learning experience.

Being patient

Social interaction takes longer to develop in a technology-based environment (Walther & Burgoon, 1992), particularly a collaborative learning environment. Learners must be allowed enough time to build a social foundation and complete their tasks. The rudiments of a community require more time to develop in online social environments than in face-to-face social environments (Tu & McIsaac, 2002); therefore, short-term online collaboration is inadequate to support the development of a community and is totally inadequate to foster community dynamics.

Active Learning

The second important construct in interactivity is active learning. Because of the blurred roles between students and teachers, more weight is placed on the learning process/experience than upon roles and "teaching" processes. Both students and teachers are learners and share their responsibilities in an online community and should be allowed a voice in determining what learning experiences they receive. Collaborative online interaction is best developed with maximum autonomy, without excessive teacher intervention and control, allowing learners to find their voices with a democratic, student-driven learning environment. Morrison (1995) suggested that the learning process is unbounded by *time* (when one learns), *space* (where one learns), *mode* (how one learns), *pace* (the rate at which one learns), *level* (the depth of learning), and *role* (with whom one learns). These conditions can be applied to online collaborative learning. Therefore, a collaborative learning community is not merely learner-centered; it is a learner-driven process when learners are granted these five conditions.

Several effective designs are introduced later in this book dealing with the interactivity dimension. Please see Chapters 4 and 5 for Design 3, Peer Support Assignment; Design 4, Interactive Project Presentation; Design 5, Online Moderation; and Design 6, Online Debate, for the design instruction and strategies.

SOCIAL CONTEXT

The second construct, social context, emphasizes the characteristics of the learner and the learner-centered social learning environment (learning community). Collaboration is inherently social (Golub, 1988; Ocker & Yaverbaum, 1999). A social group holds values regarding one's obligations to others. "Hence, people help others and/or their group because they feel it is the morally appropriate action" (Kramer & Tyler, 1996). These processes are related to the personal characteristics of online learners. Latham and Locke (1991) found that a group member skilled in self-management, goal setting, self-monitoring, and self-assessment was critical for performance. Group members in a successful group were committed to the group's mission and norms, could be counted on to perform their respective tasks, and enjoyed working in a group (Snow, Snell, & Davison, 1996). Successful online collaborative learning is an online learning community, which is an organization where community members engage intellectually, mentally, social-culturally, and interactively in various structured and unstructured activities to achieve their common learning goals through electronic communication technologies. Learners learn together and the community, itself, learns as well (Schlager, Fusco, & Schank, 2000).

Learner-Centered

Learner-centered issues are independence (the opportunity to make choices), competence (ability and skills), and support (both human and material) (Baynton, 1992). Learner-centered education has been mistakenly thought to mean leaving online learners alone, passing all responsibilities to them, and denying them appropriate communication. Online learners demonstrate higher levels of independence in learning; but their competence and technological expertise should be considered and appropriate support provided to assure a richer learning environment. Inadequate analysis of these three components may result in online learners failing and dropping out of the online instruction.

Are students ready to be accountable for their own education through collaborative learning? The fact is that many of them are not ready (Tu, 2003). How often have we heard "Can I do a personal project instead of team project?" "It is unfair on grading." "It always ends up certain people (students) are doing the work for the entire team." Or "I want to earn an A from this class and I don't want to let someone else affect my class grade." When learners ask these questions or make disparaging comments, it reveals that they do not see the value of collaborative learning, underscoring the necessity of explaining its purpose and its values at the beginning of the course.

In collaborative learning environments the teachers are learners as well. Are teachers ready for collaborative learning? Perhaps not many teachers will say yes. Most teachers may see the value of collaborative learning but they are reluctant to collaborate with other teachers, scholars, and content experts because of a fear of failure, the time involved, or being unfamiliar with online collaborative learning instructional designs.

Community

The broader view of "community" has been defined as a place where people conduct community activities, share common beliefs, and share a means of communicating (Brooks, 1997). Gilbert (2002) stated that education at Massachusetts Institute of Technology (MIT) requires a combination of the content in conjunction with a faculty member and, the critical element, the learners, mixed together in an environment that provokes inquiry and provides useful facilities to support knowledge development. This reflects the importance of learning communities.

When learning activities and interactions occur electronically, the resulting environment is referred to as an online learning community. Researchers are now advancing toward the definition of a community that learns, retains, and evolves knowledge (Tu & McIsaac, 2001). How learners gather and apply appropriate information to knowledge construction is more critical than simply obtaining information; thus, examining knowledge construction in an online community and advancing it to the level of a community that learns, rather than a location where information is simply shared and individuals learn together.

A "learning community" is decidedly different from "community learning." Several researchers (Schlager et al., 2000; Tu & McIsaac, 2001) agree with this argument (Graham, 1997). A learning community is seen as a community for participants to learn together where learning is gained horizontally. In comparison, in community learning, learning is gained both horizontally and vertically. Community members learn and the community itself also learns. Both types of learning are critical because community growth and development and the learning of community members enhance each other. Therefore, the model that stretches learning from a school learning community to lifelong learning is a good example of the relationship between the learning community and community learning.

Full community integration should advance beyond just a team community. It is difficult to draw a boundary between communities. Team members learn from various communities. With advanced technologies, team members are exposed to a greater number of related communities that provide richer perspectives for learning. The course itself is a community. With appropriate design, learners can expand their communities across courses, programs, schools, districts, regions, and countries.

Trust is one of most important social context factors. Trust influences interpersonal relationships in social interaction (Bruffee, 1995; Tu, 2002). Different forms of trust have been defined: affective, cognitive, behavioral, or "integrated" (Cummings & Bromiley, 1996; Mayer, Davis, & Schoorman, 1995; McAllister, 1995). One accepted definition of trust is: "the willingness of a party to be vulnerable to the actions of another party based on the expectation that the other will perform a particular action important to the trustor, irrespective of the ability to monitor or control that other party" (Mayer et al., 1995, p. 712). Jarvenpaa, Knoll, and Leidner (1998) stated that trust is based on the expectation that others will behave as expected; therefore, trust is a type of perception.

Community of Practice (CoP)

Communities of practice (CoPs) are groups of people who share similar goals, interests, and practices and, in doing so, employ common practices, work with the same tools, and express themselves in a common language. Through such common activity, they come to hold similar beliefs and value systems (Collaborative Visualization (CoVis) Project, 2000). These professionals are informally bound to one another through exposure to a common class of problems, a common pursuit of solutions, and, as a community, embody a store of knowledge (Peter+Trudy Johnson-Lenz, 2000). A common sense of purpose and a real need to acquire the knowledge of each other holds these professionals together. Members of CoP collaborate directly, use one another as sounding boards, and teach each other. They are not merely peers exchanging ideas who share and benefit from each other's expertise, but members committed to jointly develop better practices for the organization. Thus, developing a "community that learns" is as critical as developing a "community of learners."

Knowledge sharing is a process to guide someone through our thinking or use our insights to assist them in seeing their own situation better. Communities of practice (CoPs), one of the knowledge-sharing concepts, enables the employees to be conducive to mastery of new knowledge (Lieberman, 1996) in organizational learning and has become a cornerstone of the knowledge strategy of leading organizations (McMaster, 1999; Renyi, 1996). Several successful reform projects applied to learning organizations have supported this concept (National Science Foundation, 1997; Stokes, Sato, McLaughlin, & Talbert, 1997). Although CoP is not a new concept, we have little experience in how to foster this type of organic organizational learning community, particularly integrating electronic communication into CoP construction. In fact, Sharp (1997) suggested that improved learning would often come from encouraging development both of CoPs and CMC communities of discourse.

Electronic media are pervasively applied to employees' daily work. With the popularity of e-learning in the workplace, employees are able to learn anywhere and anytime to advance their work-related knowledge and skills. Applying e-learning empowers CoPs to extend beyond the local environment and become global. Yet understanding how these largely informal, voluntary, and self-organizing communities actually work via electronic media presents a challenge for organizations. Without an understanding of their dynamics and composition, community initiatives can be wasteful, ineffective, or even harmful.

Two relevant theoretical frameworks, McDermott's (2000) Four Key Challenges of CoP and Tu and Corry's E-Learning Community (2002), address important issues in designing online CoPs.

Four Key Challenges of CoP

McDermott (2000) proposes four key challenges in building, sustaining, and enabling CoPs to conduct effective knowledge sharing. The four key challenges are the Management Challenge, the Community Challenge, the Technical Challenge, and the Personal Challenge. The Management Challenge describes the structures and organizations necessary to guide and lead knowledge generation, sharing, and retention. The Community Challenge is the creation of real values for the community that bonds the members and coherently sustains the life of communities. The Technology Challenge is the design of knowledge management systems that ensure effective information exchange, capture, and retention in a reusable form and to reflect upon and stimulate complicated human thinking. Finally, the Personal Challenge focuses on the relationships between/among community members. These four keys should be nurtured, cared for, and legitimized to ensure that support systems are not too strenuous for the community to lose appeal for the members and not too little to allow the community to wither.

E-Learning Community

Tu and Corry (2002) propose "Instruction," "Social Interaction," and "Technology" as three major dimensions for e-learning communities. To develop an ideal e-learning community, the three dimensions should be consistently maximized. Piecemeal development may alter learning experiences. However, balanced development is a dynamic force. The development of e-learning communities may focus on different dimensions at different times, situations, and opportunities. The community may start with a greater focus on social interaction and technology. Once the community is formed, instruction can be integrated to facilitate communications. As the community develops, its influence increases and expands outward. This theoretical framework for e-learning communities is dynamic, not static; flexible, not fixed; and negotiable, not pre-set.

The effective designs to support this dimension can be found in Chapters 6, 7, and 9 and Design 7, Virtual Experts, Design 8, Guest Moderators, Design 9, Building CoP, Design 10, Electronic Media for CoP, Design 15, Understanding Social Context, and Design 16, Optimizing Online Interactivity.

TECHNOLOGIES

Technologies function as major tools in human learning. Electronic computing and telecommunications are converging into human communication and knowledge development technologies. Technology not only delivers content (information), but it has the capability to stimulate opportunities for knowledge development. Many people prefer computer technology communication tools, such as computer-mediated communication (CMC), to face-to-face communication. Technologies, such as e-mail, threaded discussion board , listserv, and real-time discussion, are powerful tools for human communication and to bring people together. This is true in education communication as well. In fact, contents, bits, learning, and cognitive science are converging into "knowledge media" (Eisenstadt, 1995). Cooper and Robinson (1998) identified technology as the most important issue in small-group learning. The technology-based instruction may have a profound impact on student outcomes. Simply making technologies available for learners is not enough for nontraditional learners in the online collaborative learning process (Ocker & Yaverbaum, 1999; Tu & Corry, 2002). Therefore, appropriate technical designs of computing technologies become critical. CMC and knowledge management systems are discussed here to address how technologies should be applied to online collaborative learning.

Computer-Mediated Communication (CMC)

Keegan (1993) declares, "Without a medium of communication the concept 'distance education' would not be an educational process. . . . Both synchronous and asynchronous media are viable means of communication for distance education . . . [and] allow two-way communication" (p. 118). Discussing quality and access in online learning from theoretical constructs, Garrison (1993) states that the "concern for quality in distance education has identified an emerging paradigm based upon two-way communication as a necessary and central component of an educational transaction" (p. 17). In other words, interactive two-way communication is the critical component in online learning. CMC has been considered one of the most effective media for online learning.

CMC technologies can be classified as synchronous (real-time communication) or asynchronous (time-delayed communication) systems (Gunawardena & McIsaac, 2003; Walther & Burgoon, 1992). Asynchronous communication does not require participants to be communicating at the same time or in the same place, for example, electronic mail, electronic threaded discussion boards, and listservs. Synchronous communication requires participants to communicate at the same time, that is, real-time computer conferencing.

A recent analysis (Tu, 2000) reveals that CMC systems enhance *and* inhibit online interaction. The user's perceptions and the attributes of CMC must both be taken into consideration (Gunawardena, 1995) because each of them has different attributes, which may impact online learning differently (Tu, 2002). The successful use of CMC in the classroom requires the selection of the correct CMC medium. CMC does not replace face-to-face communication; however, CMC provides a more flexible delivery and a greater selection of communication channels for online learners.

CMC technologies should be examined extensively. Sharing thinking patterns and using these patterns among virtual learning communities should be a central practice. Valuable information about past project history generated by an individual is not captured, retained, or maintained in a useable format to enrich the community (Tu & McIsaac, 2001). Therefore, if an individual leaves the community, the community returns to where it started and considerable time and resources may be required to reconstruct the lost knowledge or expertise. Weiser and Morrison (1998) pointed out the importance of retaining knowledge, a concept that was emphasized almost 60 years ago by Bush (1945). The ability to capture thinking trails is crucial in future thinking devices so that individuals and groups can trace the ramifications of the thought processes and learn from it by examining their own thinking. This would lead us to the development of techniques of electronic knowledge management.

Knowledge Management

An additional advantage of communication technology is its ability to be used as an extension of human knowledge. Knowledge cannot be created from emptiness. The foundation of current human knowledge is previous knowledge and maintaining knowledge for re-use is a critical issue in online learning. Therefore, a tool that is able to assist in the preservation and extension of human knowledge is important.

When using knowledge construction technologies, one should move beyond a forum for exchanging tidbits and opinions to structures that readily capture knowledge-value and foster rapid accumulation and growth of a community's capabilities (Schlager et al., 2000). For example, a technology should have the capacity to capture and index knowledge construction processes and patterns and allow users to retrieve and manipulate information from the knowledge data bank. In that manner, an online community can lead to the development of personalized, self-adaptive learning systems. In an ideal online community the contributions that are made by one member should be readily located and retrieved by other members. The processes involved in contributing knowledge and locating and retrieving it are keys to knowledge mining and knowledge construction. Knowledge becomes an emergent property that transcends the fixed-size-and-space concepts of media and information. It transcends the notion that one can impart knowledge to learners by filling them up from the teacher's vessel.

Effective knowledge management can lead to significant improvements in learner performance. A community that can effectively manage its knowledge assets is able to treat the knowledge component of learning activities as an explicit concern of learning reflected in strategy, policy, and practice at all levels of the learning environment. Tu and Corry (2002) proposed five steps to implement a knowledge management solution: (a) identify the essential elements of knowledge management; (b) assess infrastructure by evaluating the network, computer systems, security, and information; (c) anticipate the new roles of the knowledge officers, managers, or administrators, and their responsibilities; (d) select the right tools, technologies, and partners to ensure scalability and usability, and (e) support and adopt realistic collaboration. Tu and McIsaac (2001) stress the importance of knowledge management tools for online learning, making a direct connection between both explicit (recorded) and tacit (personal know-how) intellectual assets. In practice, knowledge management often encompasses identifying and mapping intellectual assets within the learning environment, generating new knowledge for competitive advantage within the learning environment, making vast amounts of information accessible, sharing the best practices, and implementing technologies that enable all of the above, including groupware, database, intranets, etc. Discovering the important factors that have an impact on the knowledge construction process should occur in future research. In addition, the selection and use of appropriate technologies to support the process is also critical.

Chapter 8, Technology, includes three designs that will provide more details regarding the appropriate applications of technologies. These designs are Design 12, Communication Technology; Design 13, Collaboration Tools; and Design 14, Selecting Appropriate Online Communication.

ASSESSMENT IN COLLABORATION

Online collaborative learning is an effective instructional design to enhance learning and training. The issue of how to evaluate online collaborative learning has been critical and challenging. Many researchers and practitioners have not reached an agreement on effective ways to assess learners' educational gains in the collaborative learning process, particularly in an online environment. Which assessment is more appropriate for collaborative learning, a group grade or an individual grade? Traditionally, instructors apply summative evaluation methods to assess the end-product and provide one grade for all team members. When a team grade is applied, learners opine that some team members contribute more to the team's work than others and a single team grade is unfair. We have all heard learners comment that doing collaborative projects is unfair because some participants fail to be involved in team activities. Additionally, instructors are usually not participants in the collaborative processes of learners; therefore, it is difficult for them to determine a fair grade. The learning process is critical to collaborative learning. Online collaborative learning, unlike cooperative learning, puts more weight on the team process in addition to the end-product. If individual grades are applied, it is difficult for instructors to assess the collaborative process since instructors are not part of the process.

Current Weaknesses in Instructor Evaluation

Weaknesses exist in the traditional instructor evaluation methods for online collaborative learning. Traditionally, instructors have determined the evaluation by an appraisal of the end-products of collaborative projects and one grade is given to all team members. This method of evaluation results in concerns that must be addressed, namely: fairness of evaluation; end-product driven; teacher-centered; inability to improve collaborative skills; and less active collaboration.

Fairness of Evaluation

Commonly, one grade is assigned to all of the team members in an online collaborative learning setting. Learners often conceive that one grade applied to all team members is unfair because some members contribute more than others. It is challenging for the instructors to be fair in evaluating each individual team member because they are not likely to participate in every single activity. Unfortunately, the only evidence of collaborative learning the instructor can evaluate is the end-products.

End-Product Driven

Traditional formative evaluations, such as a final examination, are unable to assess online collaborative learning because online collaborative learning accentuates the process of learning in addition to the product of learning. Therefore, simply applying summative (evaluating the learning process) evaluation methods to assess the end-products of online collaborative learning is inaccurate.

Teacher-Centered

Traditional evaluation methods for collaborative learning are teacher-centered because instructors predetermine the evaluation norms and evaluation methods. In other words, it is norm-referenced rather than criteria-referenced. Learners rarely are provided an opportunity to be responsible for their own learning enough to determine and negotiate how they would like to be evaluated. Falchikov (1995) stated that traditional teacher-centered evaluation systems result in conformity in learners and inhibit personal development, such as interpersonal skills. It is likely learners gain knowledge externally rather than internally.

Unable to Improve Collaborative Learning Skills

Traditional formative evaluations for collaborative learning deny learners the opportunities to improve their collaborative learning. Frequently, instructors provide a grade and feedback for the project content to the collaborative team members at the end of the project. This method does not allow learners to become aware of their own strengths and weaknesses and to improve their future collaborative learning experiences.

Less Active Collaboration

Evaluation can be more than just an examination of the learning outcome; it can be advanced to another interactive and collaborative learning experience. Conventional formative evaluation for collaborative learning occurs when learners produce a collaborative end product that the instructors evaluate, and provide feedback. The collaborators, who are most capable of evaluating the events that occurred during the production of the end product, are omitted from the evaluation process, thus limiting their interactive and collaborative learning experiences. Collaborative evaluation can be advanced to maximize the level of interaction.

Weaknesses in Student Evaluation

Although instructor evaluation has weaknesses, student evaluation has a few concerns as well. Rowntree (1987) identified eight "side-effects" of student assessment: (1) the prejudicial aspect of assessment; (2) the student's knowledge and capability of the assessment; (3) the extrinsic rewards of assessment; (4) the competitive aspect of assessment; (5) the bureaucratic aspect of assessment; (6) the nature of specific assessment techniques; (7) the giving of grades; and (8) the reporting of assessment results. The effect of these when applied to an online collaborative learning assessment is even more critical because online collaboration heavily relies on online communication that has potential for miscommunication due to the absence of facial contact.

Falchikov (1986) suggests three alternatives to traditional forms of assessment that addressed the side-effects that Rowntree identified. They are self-evaluation, peer team evaluation, and collaborative evaluation. All three are seen as promoting a learner-centered, criterion-referenced, formative, and process-oriented approach (Somervell, 1993) that has the potential to eliminate the weaknesses when both instructor evaluation and peer evaluation are applied to assess collaborative learning.

Collaborative Evaluation

A collaborative evaluation method has the potential to eliminate the weaknesses of traditional instructor evaluation and the limitations of the peer methods. Collaborative evaluation includes self-directed evaluation, self-evaluation, peer evaluation, and instructor evaluation. This technique permits learners to take control of their learning and negotiate with peers and instructors on how their collaborative learning processes should be evaluated; it achieves more democratic and comprehensive learner-centered types of evaluations that possess distinguishable changes from traditional methods and include collaborative evaluation:

- Shifts the learning responsibility from the instructor to the learners
- Shifts from norm-referenced to criterion-referenced
- Shifts from the purely summative to a mixture of formative and summative
- Shifts from external to internal
- Shifts from the evaluation of product to the evaluation of process.

The collaborative evaluation goes beyond the process of an assessment and the end procedure of the learning. It engages learners in another active learning process and another initiation of collaborative learning while reflecting on peer evaluations and self-evaluations to further develop and improve collaborative learning skills. This process also allows learners to develop an awareness of their strengths and weaknesses while interacting with their peers.

Self-Evaluation

Self-evaluation is when learners take responsibility for their own learning and further monitor and assess their learning (Boud, 1986). Learners are empowered and encouraged to take responsibility and to monitor themselves and other sources to determine what criteria should be used in judging their work rather than being dependent solely upon instructors. Baum and Baum (1986) distinguish two types of self-assessment. The first is self-assessment where the learners make judgments and evaluate their own work. The second type of self-assessment is what they call self-determined assessment, indicating that learners determine how they want to be assessed, such as determining criteria that are related to personal learning goals, what information is to be obtained, and what resources are to be contacted rather than being solely dependent on their instructors. In fact, both assessments can be applied together to allow learners more room to negotiate and to be integrated into the online collaborative learning environment.

Both types of self-evaluations engage learners in a more learner-centered approach. They have the potential to motivate learning and improve problem-solving skills of learners (Somervell, 1993). Self-determined evaluation grants learners the ability to achieve more challenging goals because it requires learners to assume control of the instrument and learning outcome by negotiating with team members and the instructors.

Peer Evaluation

Peer evaluation is a more interactive evaluation method and instructional activity (Sluijsmans, Dochy, & Moerkerke, 1999) where learners take the opportunity to evaluate each other's learning process and provide feedback. It is frequently implemented through a collaborative team project. The contributions from peers are useful for reflections on self-evaluation because learners have an opportunity to observe their peers throughout the learning process and often have more detailed knowledge of the work of others than do their teachers (Boud, 1986). Normally, it is implemented as a more formative means of evaluation. Horgan (1991) concluded that peer evaluation leads to better understanding of the work involved and better learning outcomes in collaborative learning. Based on the peer evaluation and feedback, learners can develop their own skills of reflection and enhance their collaborative learning experiences.

Peer evaluation provides a fair evaluation for online collaborative learning since team members have opportunities to evaluate their fellow team members and make contributions to the integrated evaluations. Generally, learners perceive this combined approach as a more accurate and a more fair evaluation of team projects rather than a single grade that applies to all the members of the team. Peer evaluation is conceived to be a part of self-evaluation because peer evaluation can stimulate self-reflection that makes the self-evaluation more effective. Even though Rowntree (1987) had questions on the accuracy of peer evaluation, Falchikov (1993) found that peer evaluation correlates highly with instructor evaluation. In fact, learners tend to be more critical to their team members than the instructors.

Additionally, Bulman (1996) argued that peer assessment influences the work process through peer pressure and also operates as a release valve. Learners know going into the project that they will evaluate their peers and be evaluated by them. This causes them to work harder on the project than they might if only their grades were at stake. On the rare occasion when learners avoid their fair share of work, the other members of the group have an opportunity to reveal that problem. From her observations, Bulman (1996) concluded four important issues that are successful for peer assessment in collaborative learning:

1. Learners should be aware of the importance of team projects as a part of their intellectual development (researching, critical thinking, and writing skills) and as part of workforce training;

2. Goals and objectives need to be identified clearly for any team project;

3. Organizational skills are important (assignment of individual tasks and implementation of time-tables); and

4. Each individual has a responsibility to the team and must follow through, and that this includes a responsibility to note and address problems within the team.

Important Issues

Regardless of the types of assessments, instructor evaluation, peer evaluation, self-evaluation, and the combinations for collaborative learning, it's important to follow the guidelines that Bulman (1996) proposed:

1. Allows learners to negotiate how they want to be assessed;

2. Provide an opportunity to assess the contribution of each team member;

3. Allows practice in assessment; and

4. Integrates both qualitative and quantitative assessment formats so learners can see the difference between the two.

EVALUATIONS OF TEACHING ON ONLINE COLLABORATIVE INSTRUCTIONS

Proponents of online instruction are continuously searching for effective strategies to improve online training and learning. Practitioners and researchers have focused on designing sound online instruction, using appropriate technologies to deliver the instruction, and enhancing the effectiveness with which learners use these technologies to improve training performance. Methods for evaluating these improvements and the subsequent introduction into instructional evaluation are being investigated. Issues about evaluating online training and assisting online trainers to improve their instructional design skills and online teaching skills are important for improving online training. Evaluating teaching performance is a major consideration in improving instruction and determining suitability for promotion (Tu, Yen, Corry, & Ianacone, 2003). Peer evaluation of teaching (PET) and student evaluations of teaching (SET) represent the common methods of conducting these evaluations (Cavanagh, 1996). Three challenges exist in both methods of online teaching evaluation. They are (a) summative evaluations, such as a survey, that fail to capture the values of the process of online training; (b) the results produced from PET and SET methods yield inconsistencies (Burns, 1998; Hutchings, 1996) and create difficulties in consolidating the feedback necessary to improve training; and (c) many organizations attempt to apply criteria suitable to evaluate face-to-face instruction that may be unsuitable for evaluation in the online training environment. It is proposed that a formative and descriptive evaluation has potential to resolve current concerns that integrates PET and SET to evaluate online teaching and provide feedback to help instructors improve their online teaching skills and their online instructional design skills.

Teaching evaluations are a strategy used by teachers to assist them in improving their teaching skills and, by it, improve students' learning. Students use a survey to evaluate the instruction they receive; and, although these questionnaires remain the primary source of teaching evaluations, there is evidence that peer assessments are becoming more important (Marsh, 1987). Gould (1991) concluded that both PET and SET demonstrate strengths and weaknesses, but the relationships between PET and SET are inconsistent enough to render them insignificant (Burns, 1998; Hutchings, 1996). This phenomenon generates a challenge for consolidating PET and SET. However, applying formative and descriptive methods of evaluation may address this challenge (Keig & Waggoner, 1995). Teaching is a personal art and an individual's skills (Osborne, 1998) may be difficult to evaluate if one is not familiar with the educational beliefs and teaching philosophy of the teacher being evaluated. Simply, evaluating the course materials and observing teaching may not be enough to understand the value of the instruction. Centra (1987, 1993) and Keig and Waggoner (1994) suggested use of qualitative methods to conduct teaching evaluations. Keig and Waggoner (1994) suggested that formative peer evaluation of teaching be used alongside, but apart from, summative evaluations by students. They recommend that (a) separate formative and summative tracks exist for faculty evaluation; (b) formative evaluations include nonjudgmental assessments of teaching by colleagues and administrators; (c) faculty assume leadership in developing formative evaluation programs; (d) faculty must be trained to have the skills necessary to conduct formative evaluations; (e) formative evaluations include various techniques; (f) institutional rewards recognize faculty members who participate; and (g) research be conducted on formative peer evaluation in several areas, including documentation and reporting of evaluation experiences.

It is important to understand the reasons necessitating the use of formative and descriptive evaluations. Osborne (1998) suggested five basic assumptions while conducting the integration of teaching evaluations:

1. There is no single model of teaching and learning; diversity is desired.
2. Qualitative information provides richer, more useful, feedback for improving teaching practices.
3. Peer and student evaluations of teaching can be integrated, a collaboration. By working together, the peer and the student evaluators can develop a collective meaning about the teacher's effectiveness.
4. The classroom should be a learning community that is open and capable of change.

5. In deciding about long-term retention, it is essential that we use qualitative assessment to gain a deeper understanding of the faculty member's instructional practice and its influence on students.

FUTURE ISSUES

There are a few issues to be pondered regarding the future of the online collaborative learning community (OCLC). The literature presently available has not clearly addressed these issues although some studies have touch on them (Cooper & Robinson, 1998).

1. How does online collaborative learning impact women and minority learners?
2. How should groups be formed, how large they should be, and how long should they stay together?
3. What effective strategies can be used to build an "online" collaborative learning "community"?
4. How should the freeloader/dominator issue be addressed, and how to grade when small groups are involved?
5. What are the best methods to assess an online collaborative learning community?

REFLECTIONS

In this chapter, theories and research related to collaborative learning, online learning, and community learning are presented. Technology-based online collaborative learning communities appear more complicated than face-to-face environments. It is likely that one may feel overwhelmed while implementing the concept of online collaborative learning community into classroom teaching. The purpose of this chapter is to provide background on the theoretical framework; therefore, solid rationales can be applied to develop a better understanding of the OCLC. If readers would like to explore more theories concerning this subject, the literature cited in this chapter is a good starting point.

Three theoretical constructs, interactivity, social context, and technology, are the foundation for the online collaborative learning community and they must be integrated into practice. They do not conflict with one another; however, it is often appropriate to emphasize that an individual construct is suited for a given individual circumstance. For example, if one is having difficulties sustaining the knowledge generated in collaborative learning, technology constructs may need to be emphasized to capture the knowledge generated and to sustain it for future utilization. Or, when learners have difficulties working together in harmony, social contact constructs should be examined to improve the situation.

PART II

Implementation

Part II is the muscle of this book and it describes effective designs to help the readers to conduct hands-on design and implemention of an online collaborative learning community.

CHAPTER 3

Preparation

The initiation and preparation stages are critical to fostering collaborative learning. Designing an online collaborative learning community (OCLC) requires a tremendous expenditure in time and energy for planning and preparation. A design that is well planned will reduce the confusion that learners may exhibit and ensures an interactive and rich learning experience. The preparation tasks include good communication between instructors and designers and collegial team preparation and communication. When learners know what to expect from collaboration, they are more likely to succeed in their online collaborative learning experiences. Both designs in this chapter should be implemented at the beginning of the course, allowing teams time to prepare, plan, organize, and manage their team activities. Generally, online communication requires more time to develop conclusions and consensus, particularly in asynchronous computer-mediated communication (CMC) than face-to-face (FTF). Ample time must be allowed for teams to plan their collaborative activities.

DESIGN 1 COMMUNICATION AND PREPARATION

Specifics

What	Instructor prepares and communicates the goals of OCLC with learners.
Who	Learners, instructor
When	Before and at the beginning of the course

How	Explain the goals and the purposes; conduct self-introduction; team formation
Technology	All learning technologies
Duration	Varies, usually no more than one week
Grade	N/A

Task 1: Explain the Goals and Purposes

At the beginning of the course, the instructor should explain the concept, purposes, and expectations of an online collaborative learning community. This assures that learners understand what is expected of them and will be appropriately motivated to sustain online collaborative learning activities throughout the course.

Here is an example of the purposes of integrating an online collaborative learning community.

- Enhance/enrich learning experiences
- Generate active online interaction
- Create sense of community to support community members
- Engage in the knowledge construction process with peers in addition to the instructor.

Task 2: Self-introduction

The process of self-introduction is necessary for the learners to become acquainted with each other and is vital to the selection of ideal team members. In an online learning community, social congruence does not occur as quickly as in a face-to-face communication environment. Learners engage in social functions mandating the selection of affable teammates based on the self-introductions. This seems to be an old-fashioned way to get to know each other but it requires planning to make this social function effective and create a healthy online community.

Strategy 1: Start with the Instructor's Biography

The self-introduction activity should begin with the instructor's biography. Instructors should open themselves to the class. The biography provided by the instructor is normally perceived as a model for the learners' biographies. If instructors share more of their personal information and are open to the class, it is more likely that the learners will follow suit. If possible, posting a picture provides a visual contact. A casual snapshot provides a more personalized touch than a formal portrait. Besides the personal picture, family portraits, vacation pictures, pet photos, new house pictures, or baby pictures are good pictures to share with the class. Please

	support for assignments; collaborative evaluation; set up technologies; and provide a checklist of tasks
Technology	E-mail, team threaded discussion board, real-time chat, and audio/video conferencing system
Duration	At least one week
Grade	No grade assigned

Teams should begin communicating and planning their team responsibilities immediately after being formed. The instructor must assume the critical task of assisting teams to manage, organize, and plan their team tasks. Team planning, organizing, and management are required at the very beginning of the course and it is necessary to report evidence of these activities to the instructor, such as team goals, policies, procedures, etc. Below are a few important tasks that teams should accomplish. In this process, learners should be granted with full autonomy. The results and decisions that teams make should be reported to the instructor.

Task 1: Exchanging Contact Information

Team members should exchange their contact information, such as e-mail, phone number, mailing address, personal website, etc. Each team should determine the best tool for the team to communicate during the collaboration. Frequently, learners select e-mail as their main contact tool. It is important to advise learners to exchange alternative e-mail contacts. Alternative e-mail contacts will reduce the e-mail problems caused by technology failure.

Task 2: Building Team Relationships

It is important to have the team build a collegial team relationship. The instructor should encourage team members to get acquainted with their teammates. The designated communication technologies should be available for all team members, such as a threaded discussion board and real-time chat. These communication technologies should have access only for the team members to ensure private communication.

Task 3: Team Administration

Teams should discuss their goals, policies, and procedures to ensure that they are adequately administered to achieve and complete team responsibilities assigned during the course. These administrative decisions do not necessarily need to be formal as long as all the team members agree with the decisions. There is no need for the instructor to be involved in this process. It is important that the instructor require each team to provide a copy of the team administrative document as a record. The instructor can remind teams about important issues to be covered in the team administrative discussions; such issues as "Should teams have team leaders?" "How should work be delegated to team members?" "How can team members support each other?" and "How can we achieve tasks effectively and efficiently?"

Task 4: Signing Up for Moderation

After the team is formed, it is necessary to select a lesson to moderate if team moderation is integrated (see Chapter 5, Design 5). The instructor should direct the teams in the selection of appropriate lessons to moderate. Below are a few tips that the instructor can provide to assist learners with the selection of an ideal lesson to fulfill their moderation responsibility.

- Select a lesson that is interesting to team members.
- Select a lesson that is scheduled at a time convenient for each team member. If a member of the team has an obligation during the time the selected topic is scheduled, another topic should be selected.
- Teams should be free of other obligations during the moderation period because moderation requires a commitment of time and energy.
- It is highly recommended that teams volunteer more than once for the moderation responsibility.

The instructor should allow teams to change their moderation schedule if possible. Online learners generally have other commitments; therefore, the instructor should be flexible and considerate of the learner's personal needs.

Tips

Encourage teams to sign up for moderation as early as possible and be flexible in allowing them to change their moderation schedule. Do not make moderation assignments.

Task 5: Administrations for Peer Support Assignments

If the Peer Support Assignment design (see Chapter 4, Design 3) is integrated, teams should discuss the deadlines for the first draft of assignment and the peer feedback, the format of peer evaluation, etc. Teams should discuss the appropriate deadlines for the first draft of an assignment and the peer feedback, in addition to the technology that teams will use to exchange assignments. The format of peer evaluation should be covered as well. It is important for all team members to be clear on the definition of acceptable peer feedback. This will ensure that team members are clear on providing useful and practical feedback to their peers, allowing learners to take full advantage of this design to support each other and improve their assignments.

Task 6: Collaborative Evaluation

Teams also need to negotiate, discuss, and determine how they would like their team project to be evaluated. In the design of Collaborative Evaluation (Chapter 10, Design 17), three different types of evaluations are combined to form team project evaluations: instructor evaluation, peer evaluation, and self-evaluation. In this design, 50 percent of the grade is assigned as instructor evaluation while the other half is designated for peer evaluation and self-evaluation. Teams need to negotiate how they would allocate the latter two evaluations. The decision should be made with the agreement of the entire team. A copy of the percentage allocations decided upon should be submitted to the instructor for the class record. Since this collaborative evaluation will not take place until the completed team project is evaluated, it is important that the instructor should allow teams to alter their percentage allocations if they choose to do so.

Task 7: Set up Technology

Teams require various technologies, such as communication technologies and collaboration technologies (see Chapter 8) to complete their collaborative tasks. These must be readily available. Instruction, support, and assistance setting up these technologies for team use should be provided as well.

Task 8: Provide Checklist

A checklist for team preparation is useful to ensure that all tasks are completed. The instructor should provide a clear checklist for teams to ensure they have completed their team administrative tasks. Here is an example of such a checklist.

Figure 3.1
Checklist for the Online Teams

Activity	Deadline	Report to Instructor
Exchange contact information	N/A	No.
Team administration (team goals, policies, procedures in place)	1/20/04	Yes. E-mail the instructor as an attachment.
Sign up for moderation	1/25/04	Yes. Use online submission.
Peer support for assignments	1/30/04	No. Post a copy on the team discussion board.
Collaborative evaluation	1/20/04	Yes. E-mail.
Set up technology	1/20/04	No.

> **Tips**
>
> The instructor may drop in on any team discussion sessions to ensure that teams are moving on the right track. In fact, it is important that the instructor should participate in team discussions at least once during the course and give equal support to all teams. Additionally, it is important that teams should be aware that the instructor is available and participating in their team discussions. Teams can invite the instructor to join their discussions to resolve team issues, particularly when they need guidance to complete team tasks.

REFLECTIONS

In this chapter, two major designs are introduced. Remember, it is important for the instructor to be prepared and to communicate with learners. Frequently, the instructor lacks good communication with learners and begins the course by requiring learners to perform team tasks. When time is spent introducing learners to the designs of an online collaborative learning community (OCLC), they will have appropriate and correct expectations and are more likely to know what to do and how to get projects done in more effective and efficient ways. Preparation takes the guesswork out of the OCLC process and allows experiences to be more meaningful and much less painful. After the instructor initiates effective communication, internal communication within the team can proceed without difficulty. When preparation is adequate, the instructor may not have much to do for the teams except provide encouragement and support with useful tools, strategies, guidance, etc.

CHAPTER 4

Collaboration, Interactive Assignments

The online collaborative learning community (OCLC) engages learners in active learning that includes different collaborative assignment activities to assess if they are attaining the learning objectives. Very often, assignments and class projects are designed as individual activities that require learners to work alone with limited or no support from classmates; but when they are allowed to obtain support from peers, assignments become social exercises and additional learning processes occur while maintaining the original purpose. This may enhance assignment performance and will permit the addition of peer evaluation activities. In this chapter, two designs—Design 3, Peer Support Assignment and Design 4, Interactive Project Presentation—are introduced to engage learners in active assignment and project activities.

DESIGN 3 PEER SUPPORT ASSIGNMENT

Specifics

What	Individual assignment with team supports
Who	Learners
When	Depends on the assignments
How	Explain the format; produce first draft; read peer's draft; provide peer feedback; revise the first draft; submit the final draft to the instructor
Technology	E-mail, FTP, team threaded discussion board, Digital Drop Box

| **Duration** | Depends on the assignments |
| **Grade** | No grade assigned for assignment support since this is an oblig-ation among team members. Grade is assigned for the final draft. |

Course assignments and individual projects have traditionally been a solo endeavor. Learners worked individually and obtained limited support. Here learners are allowed the benefit of peer support without sacrificing the original purpose of the assignment. In addition to engaging learners in their assignments, collaborative peer evaluation is added to enhance their assignment performance.

In peer support assignment designs, learners produce a first draft of an assignment and the final revision. The first draft is distributed to teammates, who review and return it with constructive comments. Peer feedback is used in the preparation of the final draft, which is submitted for assessment. This design can be applied to individual assignments, projects, or other activities. There is no need to apply this design to team projects or team activities since these are already designed as a collaborative. The Design 3 collaboration involves learners in four rich learning processes: preparation of a first draft, reading a peer's draft, providing constructive feedback, and the preparation of a final revision, utilizing the comments of peers.

Task 1: Explain Format

The formats and procedures involved in peer support of assignments should be explained before any assignments occur. Purposes of peer support in assignments should be elucidated permitting learners a good understanding that more work is required for this design and that they should take full advantage of this opportunity.

Reviewing a teammate's assignment and providing peer feedback allows learners to support each other and learn from each other and the instructor. In fact, reviewing an assignment prepared by someone else provides a great opportunity to improve assignment quality and overall learning experiences.

Task 2: Accentuate Autonomy

To implement learner-centered instruction, teams should be responsible for determining the policies and procedures involved in conducting peer supported assignments, such as timelines for the first draft and the peer feedback, and the requirements to be met by peer feedback. These team discussions occur at the beginning of the course while teams are forming and discussing their team business (see Design 2). These discussions may include the deadlines for the first draft and the peer feedback, and the format of the peer feedback, such as length, etc.

Strategy 1: No Need to Set Up Deadlines for Teams

The instructor is relieved of determining the deadlines for the first draft, the peer feedback, and grading the first drafts of the assignments and the peer feedback since it is an obligation shared by team members.

Strategy 2: Be Rigid on the Final Draft Deadline

Be rigid on the deadline for the assignment; learners have been granted autonomy for their first draft and the peer feedback unless personal issues are involved, such as medical conditions, etc.

Task 3: Produce a First Draft

Learners produce two drafts of each assignment, the first draft and the last draft. First drafts of assignments are distributed to teammates via e-mail or other technologies by the deadline determined by the teams.

Task 4: Provide Peer Feedback

Teammates are obligated to review the draft and return it with constructive comments. Here is an example to guide learners in reviewing the assignments of their peers and provide useful feedback.

Figure 4.1
The Guidelines on How to Review Teammates' Assignment and Provide Feedback

- Review teammates' assignment ASAP and provide feedback by the deadline.
- If you have not received your teammates' assignments, e-mail a polite reminder to them.
- Based on the instructor's assignment evaluation criteria, you need to provide practical positive and negative feedback. Simply saying "I like your . . ." is not acceptable.
- It is appropriate to provide the teammate with recommendations for improvement. If some particular assignment requirements are unclear to you, it is recommended that the issues be discussed among teammates. If the question cannot be answered by teammates, it is necessary to consult the instructor.
- How much feedback should I provide? The length and depth of the comments you provide depends on each individual and on each assignment. Generally speaking, a couple of paragraphs to a half page are average.

Tip

You may learn something while reviewing your teammate's assignments. It is appropriate to integrate any new insights into your own assignments without plagiarizing.

Task 5: Revise First Draft

After receiving the comments from peers, each individual has an opportunity to revise the assignment based on the feedback and the reflections received.

Task 6: Submit the Final Draft

Finally, learners will submit the final draft for assessment by the deadline the instructor set up for the entire class. In this collaborative learning process, learners are engaged in these rich learning processes, developing a first draft, providing a critical review of a teammate's work, and producing a revised final draft.

Tips

It's not necessary for the instructor to grade the first draft and the feedback unless there is a need to do so. The instructor may review or compare the feedback, the first draft, and the final draft of assignments to determine the progress of the learners and may provide guidance, if necessary. However, this demands a tremendous amount of time for the instructor.

Task 7: Applying Technology

There are several technologies that can be applied to buttress the peer supported assignment design, such as e-mail, threaded discussion board, FTP (File Transfer Protocol), Digital Drop Box, etc. Please see Chapter 8 Technology for more information on each individual tool.

Task 8: Clarify Assignment Criteria

Since each team member is expected to read the assignments of other team members and provide appropriate feedback and recommendations for further revisions, evaluating peer's work and providing feedback can be challenging for learners. It is highly recommended that the instructor provide assignment evaluation criteria for each individual assignment. Teams can follow these criteria to review the drafts and provide feedback.

Tips

Although there is no need for the instructor to grade the first draft and the peer reviews, it is important for learners to submit their first drafts and the peer reviews to the instructor. The instructor should monitor and review the first drafts and the peer reviews for at least the first individual assignment because learners may misunderstand the design or may not provide practical feedback, requiring the instructor to provide guidance in assisting learners to conduct a Peer Support Assignment.

Task 9: Final Project

If the final project is an individual one, the final projects can be designed like a regular assignment, learners engaging in draft preparation, reviewing peer's work, providing feedback, and revising the product to produce a final draft.

DESIGN 4 INTERACTIVE PROJECT PRESENTATION

Specifics

What	Teams present the team projects electronically and participate in question-and-answer discussions.
Who	Learners, instructor
When	End of the team project
How	Presenting project electronically
Technology	Threaded discussion board, real-time chat, electronic slide applications, HTML
Duration	1–2 week (threaded discussion board); at least 1–2 hours (real-time chat) If there are many teams, more time is needed to conduct presentation via real-time chat technology.
Grade	Presentation grades

The integration of an online presentation format into team projects or assignments requires learners to share their team projects with the entire class, to present them online, and to defend them to their peers. This design provides a good opportunity to increase the interactivity among the learners through questioning and answering. Additionally, it engages learners in gaining a better understanding of the strengths and weaknesses of their projects.

Task 1: Format

Learners of teams should review the projects of other learners or other teams and post their comments. The learners or teams who produced the project should respond to the questions asked.

It is necessary to require learners or teams to review a certain number of projects to balance questions and answers. If necessary, the instructor may require the learners or the teams to review specific projects rather than allowing them to choose. This will eliminate the problems that some projects receive more reviews and comments than others.

Task 2: Presentation Technology

Projects can be presented either asynchronously or synchronously, depending upon the contents, the learning objectives, subjects, teaching styles, learning styles of the learners, various learning situations, availability of various communication technologies, and time. Using Microsoft PowerPoint, HTML (Hypertext Markup Language) or other authoring applications to create and conduct online presentation is effective.

Regardless of which presentation technologies are used, it is recommended, not required, that each team write a short paragraph to describe their project. These descriptions provide classmates with an overview to determine what to review and evaluate. It is particularly useful if teams have special components that they would like to point out.

Task 3: Discussion Format

Both asynchronous and synchronous discussion technologies can be applied for project questions and answers. Frequently, asynchronous technology, such as a threaded discussion board, is applied because it provides a more flexible presentation format, allowing each individual project to receive the same amount of attention. Asynchronous CMC is particularly useful for project presentations, particularly when large numbers of teams are participating in the course.

If a threaded discussion is applied, each project should have its own thread on the discussion board. This provides better organization on the threaded discussion board and the questions and the answers are in a more logical sequence.

Task 4: Grading

Grades should be assigned for questions about other team projects and for project presentations and for fielding questions. The evaluation of this presentation will be based on how well students "ask" and "respond" to questions. This provides credit to learners for their online presentations and for their comments on others' projects. Learners may not participate or engage in any online presentation and Q and A activities at all if the activity is not graded.

Task 5: Questioning

It is important for the instructor to participate in the online project presentation and defense. The instructor should make their presence known by asking questions during each project presentation. The purposes of asking learners questions about the project are:

- To allow learners to demonstrate their learning outcome,
- To assist learners in understanding their own projects,

- To provide recommendations and feedback for further revisions,
- To engage learners in critical thinking, and
- To prepare learners to justify their designs.

Strategy 1: Ask at least Two Questions

It is recommended that the instructor ask at least two questions. The first question should be more general and the second question more specific to the project contents. The general question can be posted at the beginning of the online presentation and defense. Since the instructor may not have enough time to review all projects before the beginning of the presentation, a general question will give the instructor more time to review the projects and compose the second question that is more specific to the project content.

Strategy 2: Composing Effective Questions

Effective questions will generate another interactive learning experience for learners because such questions will require teams and learners to engage in active thinking processes to obtain a better understanding of their projects and provide convincing and logical justifications. This helps learners comprehend the weaknesses and strengths of their project. Below are a few examples of effective general questions:

- Please describe three strengths and three weaknesses of your project. How will you resolve or eliminate the weaknesses?
- Please use 100 words to describe your project.
- If you have another chance to redo your project, what would you do?
- How will you assess your project?

Tips

Team electronic project presentation can be applied to the individual final projects or individual assignments. This will engage individual learners in more active learning in conducting final projects and assignments. However, the instructor should be aware of the time commitments that will be required of both learners and the instructor. When each learner has to present his or her work, the process can be long and a large amount of discussion may be generated. This has potential to overwhelm both the learner and the instructor.

REFLECTIONS

Class assignments do not need to be just "assignments" that learners produce in order to demonstrate their learning outcomes for the instructor. The concepts of student publishing and peer evaluation can be integrated to accentuate the autonomy of learners and maximize learner-centered instructions. These two designs will engage learners and teams in a more motivated learning environment because the assignments and the projects are no longer a product limited to learners and the instructor. Frequently, learners are encouraged to strive to produce better work on their assignments and team projects when they are aware that they are to be shared with others.

CHAPTER 5

Collaboration, Interactive Engagements

In this chapter, two interactive online team activities—Design 5, Online Moderation, and Design 6, Online Debate—are introduced to enhance the online collaborative learning community. Both designs require learners to work as teams to accomplish learning goals.

DESIGN 5 ONLINE MODERATION

Specifics

What	Teams moderate and facilitate online lesson discussions.
Who	Learners
When	1 to 2 weeks, depending on the length of the lesson
How	Teams compose and post discussion questions, facilitate discussions, and summarize discussions.
Technology	Threaded discussion board, real-time chat
Duration	1–2 weeks (threaded discussion board); at least 1–2 hours (real-time chat)
Grade	Moderation grade should be assigned.

The purposes of online moderation are to engage learners in active learning, to take responsibility for their own learning, to maximize online interaction to broaden learners' knowledge, and to deepen learners' understandings of the contents of the assignment. The responsibilities of moderators include stimulating discussion, adding pedagogical comment, stimulating critical thinking/discussion, and creating a summary of the discussions to maximize the benefits of online interaction.

Most learners have no online discussion moderation experience. Simply assigning them moderating tasks fails to produce an ideal learning experience. In fact, it may result in frustration for both learners and the instructor. It is important to provide learners with useful guidelines and support.

Task 1: Content in Place

Teams need time to prepare for their moderation responsibilities; therefore, lesson contents and materials should be available for the teams at least three to four days before the lesson begins. These materials should include lesson objectives, lesson materials, lectures, reading materials, and the instructor's discussion questions. If there is a concern that the lesson materials will not be available before the lesson starts, at least the lesson objectives, reading materials, and the instructor's discussion questions should be available for teams to plan their online moderations.

Strategy 1: Compose Discussion Questions

The instructor should compose the lesson questions and post them before the lesson starts. This will give the moderating team more time to prepare for their moderation duties by reading the assigned materials, reading the lesson contents, analyzing the instructor's discussion questions, and composing their discussion questions. It is necessary for the instructor to compose lesson discussions because it ensures that the learners are engaged in relevant lesson contents.

Tips

The instructor can allow the moderating team to compose all of the lesson discussion questions if it is felt that the learners are able to compose appropriate, relevant, and effective discussion questions. When this approach is applied, it is recommended that the instructor review the discussion questions composed by the team moderators before they are posted.

Strategy 2: How Many Questions?

How many questions should the instructor compose for each lesson? This is a tough question because many factors affect the appropriate number of discussion questions. Basically, the instructor should consider a few critical factors:

- How many learners are in the course?
- What are the discussion requirements? How many postings are required?

- What is the duration of the online discussions?
- How many points are assigned toward online discussions?

In general, the total number of the discussion questions for each lesson should range from four to five questions. This number is based on classes with twelve to fifteen learners, requiring two postings by each learner, and the lesson discussion lasting two weeks and applying a threaded discussion board. Two points are assigned for each lesson discussion.

Strategy 3: Team Composes One or Two Discussion Questions

Each team should be expected to compose one or two discussion questions in addition to the instructor's discussion questions. However, these one or two discussion questions contributed by the team moderators should be counted into the total number of the questions for the lesson.

Tips

The instructor should be cautious about the total number of discussion questions because when there are too many questions both learners and moderators may overwhelmed, resulting in a shallow discussion of each question and the possibility that the discussion learning experiences may not be focused on relevant lesson contents. On the other hand, when too few questions are applied, the discussions have the potential to fail to cover relevant lesson content, the threads may be too long to follow, and the learners are not provided an opportunity to select the topics that interest them.

The instructor should review the moderators' discussion questions to ensure that they are appropriate. Common mistakes team moderators make are allowing their discussion questions to overlap the instructor's questions, or the questions are unclear to the class. In this situation, the instructor may request that the team moderators rewrite the questions to avoid overlapping or redundant questions.

Task 2: Develop Moderation Guidelines and Resources

Provide moderation guidelines and resources: Since learners are inexperienced at moderation, the instructor must provide guidelines and resources that allow them to advance their moderation skills. Here are examples of moderation guidelines and resources.

Figure 5.1
Moderation Guidelines

These moderation guidelines are for your reference. The guidelines and tips provided here were compiled from the experiences of previous students and their recommendations. These guidelines must be applied within an appropriate context and may not apply to all situations.

(continued)

Moderators should assist participants in sharpening the focus of the dialogue, and help them to dig deeper into the dialogue.

1. Procedures

- Review the lesson materials.
- Compose important questions not covered by the instructor's discussion questions.
- Post one to three open-ended questions, including the questions posed by the instructor.
- Facilitate discussions, including the questions posted by the instructor.
- Post a summary of the discussions after the lesson ends.

2. Guidelines

- It is recommended that teams check the discussions as frequently as possible during the time that they are moderating.
- Identify questions or issues that haven't received a response and stimulate discussion of these.
- Make sure that all students participate regularly in the discussions. If you find that someone is not participating, it is appropriate to e-mail the person individually with a warm message and invite them to become active discussion participants.
- If you feel certain questions have been adequately discussed, you can develop and post new questions or advance the discussion to different levels in the second week of the lesson. Critical thinking is important so you must challenge yourself and challenge all of the class members.
- Generate a more social dialogue and a pragmatic dialogue. Argumentative dialogue should be avoided.
- Clarify the messages if the postings are not clear to you. Do not assume! It may cause misunderstanding. It is not necessary to press offensively.
- Ensure that participants feel welcome and safe and model the use of the virtual medium to minimize miscommunication.
- Use appropriate tones: nurturing, humorous, imaginative, neutral, curious, analytical, informal, and whimsical.
- Do not use an offensive tone: anger, irony, etc.
- A system of multiple leaders who rotate the lead can be a useful strategy to conduct team moderations.
- Summarize and synthesize postings to draw together main themes.

3. Healthy discussions will:

- Carry a sense of community;
- Encourage regular participation by community members;
- Demonstrate that the online community meets its members' needs, and the participants express honest opinions;

(continued)

> - Produce evident participant-to-participant collaboration and teaching, and spontaneous moderating will occur among the participants;
> - Permit reasonable venting about technology, content, and even the facilitator; and
> - Demonstrate that participants show concern and support for the community.
>
> 4. If you are unsure of something, consult with the instructor.

Moderation Resources

- EModerators, Berge Collins Associates
  (http://www.emoderators.com/moderators.html)
- Rohfeld, Rae Wahl, & Hiemstra, Roger. (1995). Moderating Discussions in the Electronic Classroom.
  (http://www.emoderators.com/moderators/rohfeld. html)
- Berge, Zane. (1995). The Role of the Online Instructor/Facilitator.
  (http://www.emoderators.com/moderators/teach_online)
- Collins, Mauri P., & Berge, Zane L. (1997). Moderating Online Electronic Discussion Groups.
  (http://www.emoderators.com/moderators/sur_aera97. html)

Task 3: Explain the Purposes

It is important to explain the purposes of online moderation to learners so that learners have correct expectations and are more likely to meet requirements. To novice moderators, online moderating is a challenge because learners frequently find that not being content experts prevents them from actively engaging in moderating. If learners have a better understanding of the purposes and expectations of online moderation, they are more likely to feel comfortable and confident to perform the moderation tasks.

Task 4: Sign Up

After all of the preparatory tasks are completed, teams need to sign up for one or more lessons to fulfill their moderating responsibilities. Generally, signing up for lesson responsibilities takes place in the beginning of the course so teams can prepare their moderations as early as convenient. Please see Chapter 3 Design 2 Team Goals/Objectives Setting for strategies in assisting teams to sign up for lesson moderations.

Task 5: Communications

The instructor should e-mail the team three to four days before the lesson begins or earlier to remind its members of their moderation responsibility to allow the team time to finish preparing for their moderation tasks, identifying important discussion questions composed by the teams, posting questions, and working collaboratively with teammates. In the e-mail the instructor should state the purposes and expectations of moderation and procedures of moderations.

Task 6: Assist/model Moderation

After discussions start, the instructor should continue communicating with the team responsible for moderation by e-mail to guide them through the moderation process. The instructor should provide positive feedback on questions, provide feedback on moderations, assist them to sustain discussions, and help them summarize the discussions. In other words, when this leadership is given to a team, it is imperative that the instructor provide appropriate guidance and feedback to team moderators. Alternatively, the instructor may consider co-moderating the online discussion to guide and lead novice moderators.

It is recommended that the instructor should serve as a model by moderating the first lesson discussion. This is particularly necessary if none of the learners have experience in online moderation. Modeling demonstrates ideal moderating strategies and methods to learners. Learners will gain a better idea of how to conduct online moderation.

Tips

Be positive about the moderating team's accomplishments; encourage rather than criticize.

Do not leave team moderators alone. Shifting leadership doesn't relieve the instructor of the responsibility for the discussions.

DESIGN 6 ONLINE DEBATE

Specifics

What	Learners are divided into pro and con positions to debate a contentious topic relevant to the course content via online threaded discussion board.
Who	Learners
When	The middle of the course
How	Set up goals, policy, and procedures; assign debate positions; proceed with the debate; conclude and wrap-up debates; extend post-debate analysis activities
Technology	Threaded discussion board
Duration	1–2 weeks
Grade	Debate grade should be assigned.

Online Debate

Online discussion is used extensively because it promotes several types of thinking: critical thinking, higher-order thinking, distributed thinking, and constructive thinking (Berge & Muilenburg, 2000). The type of thinking to be stimulated determines the discussion method used. Online discussion is not limited to learners reading assigned materials and responding to questions posted by the instructor. Online debate presents an alternative discussion strategy in computer-mediated communication (CMC). This design describes the development of a semi-structured online debate to enhance online learning and online training by asynchronous CMC technology.

Debate is a maneuver where learners are divided onto opposing sides, generally as teams, to dispute a contentious issue. Learners are afforded the opportunity to improve their analytic and communication skills by formulating ideas, defending positions, and critiquing counter positions. Historically, a debate is a structured activity; however, online media permit a wider range of designs for online debates, from an inflexibly structured exercise to a process with minimal structure. When an online debate is more rigid, step-by-step instructions are provided for debate and defense, as in a formal face-to-face debate. When online debate is designed with less structure, it operates as an online discussion concerning a controversial issue. In this design, a semi-structured online debate is proposed to implement online deliberation. Basically, online learners (debaters) are assigned a particular issue and are prepared to assume a pro or con position. Debaters are assigned a position and are expected to defend and justify that position. The design is meant to encourage online learners to exercise critical thinking, to consider both sides of an issue, and to appeal to the sensitivities of others. It is not intended to degrade traditional online discussion. In fact, the intention is to identify potential and alternative effective online instructional design strategies.

Goals of Online Debate

Online debates have four goals: construct meaningful knowledge, engage in comprehensive speculation, enhance learner-learner interaction, and develop skills in persuasive argument.

Constructing Meaningful Knowledge

The primary goal of an online debate is to focus the attention of learners on the interactive construction of meaningful knowledge and apply it to novel situations rather than acquiring and memorizing information (Schaeffer, McGrady, Bhargava, & Engel, 2002). The debating process requires participants to obtain and construct meaningful arguments to justify/defend their positions. Fragmented information or knowledge will place debaters in a vulnerable position.

Engaging in Comprehensive Speculating

Training learners in the skills necessary to view an issue from multiple aspects is critical. One purpose of online debates, distinguishing them from online discussions, is engaging learners in observing an issue from multiple points of view, unlike online discussions that permit learners to discuss issues from the aspect of their own preferred thinking. Since online debate may assign learners to either side of an issue, learners must research and speculate the strengths and weaknesses of both sides in order to strengthen their positions, defend the weaknesses of the opinion they are defending, and expose the weaknesses of the opposing position. This engagement obliges learners to establish a broader understanding of the issue being debated.

Enhancing Learner-Learner Interaction

The structured, threaded, online debate forum is designed to enhance learner-learner interaction and encourages learners to make reasoned, persuasive, and concise arguments in areas where precise answers do not exist. This is an example of reflections on real-world issues that are ill-structured and complicate the factors that contribute to the actual issue. In fact, learners are strongly engaged in learner-learner interaction because debaters must cogitate every posting and make an opposite reaction.

Developing Skills in Persuasive Argument

An important goal of online debates is to improve the ability of learners to argue persuasively. Unlike most online discussion formats, an online debate appoints learners to actively engage in discussions of certain controversial issues and through contention attempt to persuade their peers to embrace their viewpoint (Engel & Schaeffer, 2001). The more effective learning outcome is that learners are able to solidify their opinion of the issue, or adopt a new opinion, while persuading others to adopt their assigned side of the issue.

Online discussion methods are not limited to learners reading assigned materials and responding to questions posted by the instructor. Online debate is an effective discussion method for engaging online learners in a more interactive method of constructing meaningful knowledge. This design discusses the use of a semi-structured online asynchronous debate to improve the analytic and communication skills of online learners through formulating ideas, defending positions, and critiquing counter positions. Important and practical guidelines for designing effective and successful online debates are listed below. The guidelines are organized into three stages—preparation, debate, and finalizing—utilized in asynchronous CMC technology, such as threaded discussion in online debate.

Most tasks should be completed in the preparation stage. In other words, good preparation will assure the success of the online debate.

Task 1: Preparations

The preparation occurs well before the actual debate begins. The instructor and instructional designers devise detailed formats, rules, and procedures. Comprehensive preparations will help eliminate confusion for the learners and help ensure a successful online debate.

Strategy 1: Setting Debate Objectives

The instructor or the instructional designer should start by determining the objectives to be achieved through the online debate. This is when one reviews the four goals of online debates, discussed earlier. All four goals should be integrated into the design; however, depending upon the context, the instructor or the instructional designer may want to emphasize one or more of these goals.

Strategy 2: Select Debate Topics

The debate topic should be clear, authentic, and accompanied by appropriate statements and examples relevant to the debaters. The topic and its wording are instrumental in encouraging or discouraging active debate. Debaters are apt to be more engaged with authentic issues with which they can personally relate and can see addressed in the larger social context. A good topic would: be controversial; allow debaters to take multiple positions, without one obvious best; contain enough complexity to allow it to be interpreted from multiple perspectives (e.g., stakeholders) and from multiple disciplines; and be relevant to learners. After a topic is determined, it should be stated as both pro and con positions. For example: Should the curriculum be standardized for all students? The pro position: The curriculum SHOULD be standardized for all students. The con position: The curriculum SHOULD NOT be standardized for all students.

Strategy 3: Determine Debate Format

Debate formats are determined depending upon the degree of structure that one wishes to impose. The format can range from formal (more structured) to informal (less structured) and may be a mixture of formal and informal formats. The formal debate refers to a more structured design, such as parliamentary debate, while an informal debate will appear more like an online discussion and conversation format on a controversial topic. This design describes a semi-structured online debate that applies mixtures of formal and informal debate formats.

A semi-structured online debate allows one to regulate the opening and closing statements for the debates. Both sides are required to post their opening and closing statements on a designated date. Between opening and closing statements, the floor will be open for free debates. During the open debates, there is no limit on the number of messages and no pre-scribed sequence for posting debate messages.

Strategy 4: Devise a Timeline

The timeline applied depends upon the form of CMC used, synchro-nous or asynchronous. Clearly, synchronous debate is analogous to regu-lar face-to-face debate. The difference is that debaters are required to type rather than speak. Asynchronous debate is a new arena for debating. The characteristics of asynchronous communication allow debaters more time to prepare their responses. A period of at least one week of debate should be allowed and, when time permits, a period of two weeks is appropriate. Debates may become less focused if more than three weeks are allotted. It is more challenging for the debaters to concentrate their logistical rea-soning. It generally takes longer for asynchronous debaters to prepare their messages, but they tend to be more thoughtful, more logical, and have more evidence to support the arguments. This is important that one should devise timelines for online debates.

Strategy 5: Supply Supporting Materials

Providing resource locations on both positions is vital. The instructor or the debate moderators should direct the debaters to relevant resources before and during the debate; therefore, the debaters are equipped with facts and knowledge to justify their deliberations. Additional debate resources should be provided as well. In fact, a debate resource database can be established for the debate. Debaters, moderators, and the instruc-tor can contribute additional resources to the resource database through-out the entire debate process.

Strategy 6: Establish Rules

Guidelines are important to debaters because they state the instructor's expectation for the debate. Debate can be an intimidating process for those without experience in debating; therefore, the rules and guidelines must be detailed and descriptive. There are at least three types of guide-lines to be prepared and provided: The debate guidelines, the conduct of online debates, and the debate moderation guidelines when learner mod-eration is applied. The debate guidelines should state clearly the duties, procedures, expectations, strategies, and tips. The conduct of an online debate regulates acceptable debating behaviors. Misconduct during the debate is most likely to occur because text-based CMC lacks nonverbal cues. Misunderstanding the plain texts with lean channels of communications could trigger flaming behavior. The moderation guidelines should communicate the roles and tasks of the moderator. Please see Figure 5.2 and Figure 5.3 for examples of the three types of the guidelines.

Figure 5.2
Online Debate Instructions

Asynchronous Online Debate (6 Points)

Form: Team Activity
Time: Lesson 4 (Two weeks)
Objectives:

- To obtain comprehensive understanding of multiple views of an issue.
- To critically assess and present the evidence and resources of the debate topic.
- To convince the audience that your position is the most reasonable.

Debate topic:
Is online collaborative learning environment able to foster sociability?

PRO: Online collaborative learning environments CAN foster sociability.
CON: Online collaborative learning CANNOT foster sociability.
Teams will be assigned with Pro or Con by the instructor.

Rules:

Deadline
Tasks
10/06/03

- Moderators cast their vote on either Pro or Con.
- Moderators post the introductory statement of the debate topic (500 words).

10/08/03

- Both Pro and Con sides post one opening statement (500 Words).

10/09/03–10/16/03

- Open debate. The numbers of postings and the lengths of postings are unlimited.

10/17/03

- Both Pro and Con make Rebuttals (500 words)

(continued)

10/19/03

- Moderators post closing statement (500 words).
- Moderators cast their final vote to either Pro or Con.

Debate Strategies

- Comprehensive research relevant issues
  - To develop persuasive arguments, debaters need to research and consider the relevant issues involved in both positions rather than just their position.
- Strengths and weaknesses of the both positions
  - Identify strengths and weaknesses of both positions.
- Perform critical and logical process
  - Critically analyze the relevant information and issues obtained on both positions.
  - Synthesize the information.
  - Present it with more persuasive form.
  - Look for weaknesses in the opposing group's arguments. Prepare strategies to refute your opponent's arguments.
  - Are the arguments relevant to the debate topics? Does the opposing group lack information to support their claims? Are the there any flaws in reasoning?
  - Know the common errors in thinking, such as logical reasoning fallacies, and use them effectively in the refutation.
  - Predict counter-arguments and demonstrate that your position is the most reasonable. In other words, turn the opposing position's weakness into your position's strengths.
- Presentation
  - Any argument, refutation, and defense should be concise and clear.
  - Be mindful of any wording because any message is permanent during the debate, unlike face-to-face debates.
- Supporting evidences
  - Present the content accurately with support from authoritative and valid sources.
  - Challenge the validity of evidence presented by the opponents.
- Coordinate team task
  - Coordinate debate partners and amalgamate the arguments to strengthen the position.
  - Support and emphasize the teammates' arguments.

(continued)

Evaluation criteria

- Afford strong and clear opening and closing statements.
- Justify the position effectively.
- Identify and reveal the opponents' weaknesses and reasoning flaws.
- Present the strong evidence to support the defending position and reveal the opponents' flaw.
- Post messages timely and accurately.
- Demonstrate the cohesion of the team during the debating position.

Conduct of debates

- Any misconduct may result in the postings being removed from the debate message board or disqualification for the debater.
- Questions or challenges should be professional and relevant to the debate topic. Insulting and offensive language is unacceptable. Any description or comment involving personal language or attacks is considered offensive.
- Debaters should avoid impugning the motives of their opponents and the moderators.
- Any debate message not relevant to the topic will be removed from the discussion board.

Debate Resources

- Introduction to the way of reason (http://debate.uvm.edu/code/001.html)
- Debate (http://www.42explore.com/debate.htm)
- Debate Central (http://debate.uvm.edu/)

Figure 5.3
The Tasks and Guidelines for the Online Debate Moderators

Tasks

1. Facilitate online debate.
2. Post an open statement that addresses the importance of the debate topic and raise the elements of the controversy.
3. Post a closing statement that summarizes the debate messages and closes the debate.
4. Support and assist both sides to develop and organize their debating strategies.
5. Limit answering administrative questions.
6. Provide advice about where to find resources and how to search for them. It is not the role of moderators to do the work for the teams.
7. Maintain and update the debate resource database.

(*continued*)

> **Guidelines**
>
> 1. It is inappropriate for moderators to participate in the creation of any work product for the teams. It may skew the debate positions.
> 2. The moderators may not participate in the actual debate; however, it is important to keep the debate focused on the relevant tasks.
> 3. Frequently private messages to the debaters are more appropriate. An announcement can be applied as well.
> 4. Remind the debaters of the consequences if they fail to participate during the debate.

Strategy 7: Establish Evaluation

The debate evaluation criteria should be stated clearly before the debate. Good evaluation criteria will inform the debaters of the expected focus and conduct of the debate. The evaluation criteria should be based on the goals of the debate; however, caution must be exercised to prevent determining the actual debate results because the purpose of a debate is to establish thoughtful processes and not to establish a solution for the topic under discussion. In fact, the preferred debate topic is a conundrum; debate is redundant if an answer is apparent. The evaluation of debates should lie in the processes of the debate rather than the results of the debate. Good evaluation criteria should focus on the intended goals and allow debaters to demonstrate their abilities:

- Ability to clarify and aid in the understanding of positions.
- Ability to identify, defend, and justify the strengths and weaknesses of a position.
- Ability to provide appropriate supporting resources to sustain the argument.
- Ability to post timely messages.
- Ability to demonstrate team cohesion on the position being supported in the debate.

Task 2: Debating

A debate includes several vital processes: announcing debate rules, grouping/assigning tasks, opening statements, facilitating, and providing timely feedback.

Strategy 1: Announcing Debate Rules

The debate should be initiated by announcing the debate rules that permit debaters to assume a proper stance during the debate process. Debate is a team activity. The learners are divided into teams.

Strategy 2: Assigning Roles

The teams are assigned a position, pro or con. If there are more than two teams, multiple pairs of debaters can be applied allowing two teams to debate each side of the issue. One team can be assigned to be debate moderators. Alternatively, the instructor can invite guest moderators who are experts on the particular debate topic.

Moderators answer administrative questions and give suggestions about how debaters might organize themselves, how to develop debate strategies, and how to prepare for the debate. It is appropriate to provide some advice about where to find resources but not to provide resources for them. The moderators must be available to give advice about where resources might be found online, how to develop a debate strategy, and what might be included in a resource abstract, etc.

Strategy 3: Polling

Before the debate begins, the moderators are polled regarding their opinions on the issue. This initial vote regarding the debate topic serves to commit them to the debate. The instructor will collect the votes from the moderators and announce the results. This is repeated after the debate is closed to determine if the debaters have been able to sway the opinion of the moderators.

Strategy 4: Introductory Statement/Opening Statements

An introductory statement by the moderators is critical to prepare both positions to recognize weaknesses in the opposing argument. The introductory statement by the moderators should be a factual observation of the question. Any prejudice conveyed in these statements may potentially skew the results of the debate and should be avoided. Opening statements follow the moderator's opening statement from both sides in support of their positions. These statements should be posted by a specific time with a defined word limitation.

Strategy 5: Open Debate

After the opening statements are posted, the floor is opened for debate by both sides and is impartially facilitated by the moderators. The open debate allows both sides to demonstrate weaknesses in the argument of the opposition and justify their own arguments. Open debate should occur without limitation on the frequency of postings or the length of postings. The debaters should be allowed to debate and justify freely within the period of time given.

Strategy 6: Debate Resources

Moderators, while following the debate guidelines, should supply authoritative resources to assist the debaters in presenting their positions concisely and professionally. Debaters are led toward in-depth exploration through the assistance of appropriate facilitation. The lectures and assigned reading materials should provide relevant background information that can be drawn into the debate, and should demonstrate the type of reasoning required to tackle the flow of the opponents' reasoning.

Strategy 7: The Role of the Instructor

The role of the instructor during the debate is to guide the debaters in attaining the objectives of the debate. The instructor remains on the sideline and does not participate in the debate. The presence of an instructor is necessary during a debate to maintain the direction of the discourse and to intervene when the debate moves in the wrong direction. The instructor should observe the debate process closely and provide timely feedback. Debaters and moderators may not be familiar with the debate process and the tactful use of effective debate strategies; therefore, the instructor is present to provide timely and constructive feedback to each team or each individual. A private communication may be necessary to avoid interference with the debate outcome because the instructor's interference may alter the balance of the debate position and skew the results. The feedback should be constructive and suggestive, not judgmental.

Task 3: Finalizing

In the final stage of the debate, several processes need to be completed in order to wrap up the debate.

Strategy 1: Closing Statement

In the final stage of the online debate, the moderators should post closing statements followed by rebuttals from both positions. The moderators' closing statement should illuminate the main points that each position presented.

Strategy 2: Polling

The moderators vote again on either the pro or con positions after the closing statements are posted. The instructor collects the votes and determines how many of the moderators were swayed to the opposite position and announces the results.

Strategy 3: Overall Comments

To wrap up the debate, the instructor should post overall comments and feedback for the entire debate. These should point out the critical issues that were not covered during the debate. It is important for the instructor to challenge the debaters to consider how the future debaters will appreciate the topic. The instructor should also provide a summative assessment of the debate based on the evaluation criteria. This assessment should be a team evaluation. Individual assessments can be applied, if necessary.

Strategy 4: Extended Activities

Extended activities are valuable additions to the online debate if time and circumstances permit, analyzing the pro and con arguments, and composing an improvement report. Each team should analyze the arguments and justifications presented by both teams to produce an after-action report addressing how future debates may be improved.

REFLECTIONS

Online debate is an alternative method utilized to enhance online learning, to encourage critical thinking, and to develop an appreciation of opposing points of view. It motivates learners to contribute and stimulates interest in what their opponents have to say. Learners actively build on each other's ideas, and at the same time introduce new elements into the discourse. With appropriate online debate design, learners become more skilled at constructing persuasive arguments and knowledge.

CHAPTER 6

Beyond the Class Community

The online community doesn't need to be limited in class communities only. In fact, we should take advantage of online technology to expand the in-class community to the external community. The online technology allows us to obtain resources, information, and support going beyond the schools and the local and stretch to the national and international. In this chapter, two designs are covered: Design 7 Virtual Experts and Design 8 Guest Moderators.

Inviting virtual experts and guest moderators to support the online learning community sounds very easy. However, without appropriate planning, the designs may suffer from miscommunication and create frustrations for learners, experts, and the instructor.

DESIGN 7 VIRTUAL EXPERTS

Specifics

What	Teams interact with virtual experts via e-mail.
Who	Learners, virtual experts
When	Throughout entire course
How	Teams e-mail the virtual experts; receive the experts' responses; share the responses with the entire class.
Technology	E-mail; threaded discussion board
Duration	Throughout entire class
Grade	No additional grade point assigned. It can be integrated with regular online discussions.

This design provides an opportunity to take advantage of online technology to obtain valuable support that is normally not available through face-to-face instruction. This design will expand the course resources beyond the class. Basically, the instructor needs to invite experts in certain subjects or topics that are relevant to the course content. Teams can consult with the experts to be exposed to their expertise and receive expert guidance and support via online technologies. This engages learners in active learning dialogues with experts. Teams should share their learning experiences from the experts with the entire class, permitting the entire class to benefit from the virtual experts' skill.

Task 1: Inviting Virtual Experts

Strategy 1: Contact the Experts

First, the instructor needs to decide which experts should be invited. These people should be the experts in topics relevant to the course content. How many experts should be invited? This is a tough question to answer. It is important to provide the appropriate number of virtual experts to prevent them from being overwhelmed. If there are too many experts for the number of teams, the experts may feel ignored. Therefore, we need to be careful on the ratio of teams to the virtual experts. There are a few important concepts that must be clarified about virtual experts because they are very busy. It is important to make this task easy for them and conserve their involvement as much as possible. This interaction must be carefully planned and clearly communicated to the experts to prevent them from being overwhelmed by the learners.

Strategy 2: Clear Instructions for the Experts

There are a few important things that need to be made clear to the virtual experts so they understand what is expected of them.

1. The role of the virtual experts is to provide suggestions, guidance, and support to the teams.
2. They need to provide contact information and a reliable time frame for responding.
3. They are responsible for two or three responses to the inquiries posed by the teams throughout the course.
4. The responses of the experts will be shared with the entire class to decrease the burden of developing responses to repeated inquiries.
5. It is appropriate to decline inquiries if the experts are unable to commit to continuing support.

The virtual experts should provide guidance and support. It is important to make it clear that the virtual expert SHOULD NOT provide direct answers to questions from the teams, but should apply the Socratic questioning approach to support the teams rather than to provide them with direct answers.

Strategy 3: Obtain Accurate Contact Information

Correct contact information is imperative for this design to be successful. The best way to bring together the teams and the virtual experts is through e-mail communication; therefore, it is necessary to obtain correct e-mail addresses from the experts. Many people have multiple e-mail accounts; therefore, obtaining the address of an appropriate e-mail account is important. It is also critical that the virtual experts determine how rapidly they are able to respond to the teams' requests. This information should be available to the class so learners have appropriate expectations about when they will receive responses from the experts.

Strategy 4: Reasonable Commitments

Each expert should be responsible for only two or three inquiries unless they are willing to spend more time with the teams. Responding to teams' inquiries can be very time-consuming, particularly by text-based computer-mediated communication (CMC). The instructor should protect the virtual experts' involvement to prevent them from being overwhelmed.

It is important to notify the virtual experts that their responses to the teams will be shared with the entire class. When the same questions or similar questions are asked by the teams, the virtual experts can refer them to the teams that have already received guidance.

Tips

One last thing, the virtual experts should be aware that they have the right to decline responding to questions if they are unable to commit to responding within the expected time limitations. It is impossible to predict the difficulties encountered in professional and personal activities; frequently, there are unexpected occurrences in their daily life that will take precedence over other commitments.

Task 2: Establish a Virtual Expert Policy

The instructor must determine policies and guidelines regarding virtual experts that are clearly understood by the learners. Simply asking learners to contact the virtual experts for support is not appropriate. There are many important issues; format, frequency, and courtesy/netiquette are among the many important issues that must be understood by the learners to make the learning experience with the virtual experts more effective and to prevent episodes that could offend the virtual expert.

Strategy 1: Establish Guidelines

The instructor should set up, announce, and explain the guidelines for contacting the virtual experts to learners, allowing them to know how to approach the virtual experts and what to expect in their interaction. An example of these guidelines for virtual experts is shown in Figure 6.1.

Strategy 2: Address the Format and Frequency

The instructor should clearly address the format used when contacting the virtual experts and the frequency with which they should be contacted. Below are the issues that need to be addressed:

- Explain the purposes of the virtual experts' activities.
- Learners should contact the experts by teams rather than individually.
- Each team should contact at least one of the virtual experts once during the course but no more than three times.
- Teams should share their responses received from the experts within a defined time period in a designated area, such as a designated threaded discussion board.

Figure 6.1
Guidelines for Communicating with Virtual Experts

The purpose of virtual experts is to enhance learning in the course content area through e-mail contact with virtual experts and obtain guidance and support beyond that available within the boundaries of the class. This opportunity allows students to expand their online learning community.

The instructor has invited several well-known scholars, professors, researchers, and administrators in the profession of educational technology as resources to ease the learning process and enrich the experience, during the course. Below is a list of the virtual experts with their names, institutional affiliation, professions, and message response time.

Students, working as a team, should contact any of the virtual experts, when desired, for more information. There is a threaded discussion board on the course website that is designated for messages from virtual experts. Teams will share the information received from their virtual expert interactions with their classmates in this designated threaded discussion area. It is NOT a required class activity; however, students should cherish this opportunity to ease their learning process and enrich their experiences through interactions with the virtual experts.

It is very important is that the communications with virtual experts be kept to a reasonable amount of e-mail exchanges. All of the virtual experts are heavily committed with professional work at their own institutions and we must

(*continued*)

appreciate their willingness to use their spare time to assist our class. Below are some guidelines that are to be followed when you contact the virtual experts:

1. Select a virtual expert whose expertise is in the field with which your questions deal.
2. Each expert is committed to two or three responses to the class. Do not overwhelm them.
3. "DO NOT" send the same questions to all of them. It is unprofessional unless there is a need.
4. While e-mailing them:
   a. Contact them as a team.
   b. Identify yourself as a team member first.
   c. Mention that you are students and provide the instructor's name.
   d. Be polite and positive.
   e. Keep your messages short and concise.
5. Respect their response.
6. If you do not understand their messages, ask for clarification politely and positively.
7. Do not "push" if you don't hear from them in a short period of time. Generally, they are very good at responding to their e-mail s.
8. At the end of the course, send them a note of appreciation.
9. Obtain permission if you would like to maintain contact with them.
10. If you don't know how to communicate with them, it is always best to consult with the instructor.

List of Virtual Experts

Name	Joe Smith; jsmoth@wau.edu
Title/Affiliation	Professor, Western Arizona University
Expertise	Knowledge Management
Turn Around Time	3–4 days
Name	Mary Wilson; mwilson@ift.com
Title/Affiliation	Researcher, InFo Technology Inc.
Expertise	Online Training
Turn Around Time	1–2 days
Name	John Murphy; Murphy@hotmail.com
Title/Affiliation	Instructional Specialist, Quest Consulting
Expertise	Learning Objectives
Turn Around Time	3 days

The instructor should reemphasize the roles of the virtual experts in addition to defining the formats used when contacting them. This will prevent misconceptions and misunderstanding by the learners.

- The virtual experts are supposed to provide guidance, not to give answers.
- It is unprofessional to ask the experts to do work for the teams.
- The best way to interact with the experts is to use them to generate inspiration.

Strategy 3: Acceptable Codes

It is necessary to define acceptable communication behaviors. Because text-based communication lacks nonverbal cues, messages should be composed with great thought. Learners should practice acceptable netiquette when they communicate with the experts.

- Learners should allow the expert time to respond. Each expert's response time is listed in the guideline. Learners should allow one to two grace days in addition to the expert's usual response time before re-contacting the expert. At that time the learner can send a friendly reminder to the expert.
- The learners should cherish the opportunities to access virtual experts.
- It is always necessary to ask permission for further questions and communications.
- Learners should be aware that the experts might not be able to respond to their questions due to other commitments.

Task 3: Meeting Exchange Corner

A threaded discussion board should be set up for learners to share and exchange the responses and guidance they receive from the virtual experts. This asynchronous board serves a few purposes; it allows learners to be aware of which experts have been contacted and what questions were asked in addition to the exchange and sharing of information. This information will eliminate overlapping questions. The instructor also can transform the information exchange into another class discussion activity to enrich learning experiences. Frequently, the experts may introduce valuable information and knowledge to the learners who ask questions. The content of the virtual experts' responses may deserve in-depth discussions.

Tips: Guest Speakers

Through the threaded discussion of the virtual experts' message exchange, the instructor may identify issues and contents that interest learners and deserve further elaboration and interaction with certain experts. The instructor can request that the virtual expert participate in the online class activities as a guest speaker, guest lecturer, or guest moderator (see Design 8, Guest Moderators). This will extend this design to a more intensive and in-depth interaction with the experts.

Task 4: Express Appreciation to Experts

It is very important to for the learners and the instructor to send the virtual experts an e-mail expressing appreciation. The experts who are not questioned should also be thanked with an e-mail that expresses appreciation from both the learners and the instructor.

DESIGN 8 GUEST MODERATORS

Specifics

What	Moderating course discussion by invited guests
Who	Guest moderators
When	Middle of the class
How	Invite guest moderators; explain the format; explain the role
Technology	E-mail; threaded discussion board
Duration	1–2 weeks
Grade	No grade assignment is necessary.

The design of Guest Moderators is an extension of Team Moderation (see Design 5) and Virtual Experts (see Design 7). This design is to invite guests to the class who are experts on certain topics to moderate the online discussion on the topics within their expertise. This design places the learners in direct interaction with experts during class discussions.

Task 1: Inviting Moderators

The instructor should contact prospective guest moderators and extend an invitation. More than one guest moderator can be used to moderate the same topic or lesson. This is particularly important when the class has a large number of learners.

Task 2: Explain the Format

The instructor should explain the online discussion and the online moderation formats, allowing the guest moderators appropriate expectations of their responsibilities. The instructor should forward the learners' online discussion policy and online discussion grading policy to the guest moderators. It may be helpful to the guest moderators to allow them access to previous online discussions. This permits the guest moderators to form an idea of how online discussions have been conducted in this particular course. If the discussion technology requires special attention, the instructor should explain how the discussion technology works or provide a tutorial. This will eliminate technical problems for the guest moderators.

Task 3: Explain the Role

The guest moderators may not be familiar with online moderation despite being experts in the discussion topics. The instructor should explain the role of online moderator. The role guest moderators play is similar to that learners play as moderators; therefore, the instructor can forward the learner online moderation guidelines (see Chapter 5, Design 5, Team Moderation) to guest moderators.

Tips: Instructor's Presence

Although the instructor delegates the authority of online discussion moderation to guest moderators, the instructor's presence in the online discussion is crucial. In fact, delegating moderating responsibility to a guest doesn't relieve the instructor from the responsibility of participating in online discussion activities. The instructor should monitor the discussion by observing the interaction between the guest moderators and the learners. The instructor may need to intervene to ensure that the discussion is on the right track. Commonly, a discussion involving a guest moderator dissolves into a question-and-answer format, where learners ask questions and the guest moderators simply provide answers, rather than engaging in critical thinking and discussion. This situation can be avoided when the instructor participates in the discussions and shifts the discussions to a more ideal engagement.

REFLECTIONS

Online learning is not limited only to in-class communities. In fact, a good instructor should take advantage of computer technologies and seek opportunities for external support and resources to build external learning communities. Through the application of computer technologies, the instructor can bring together learners and external resources to enhance online learning by stimulating more ideal interactions. This is another example where the instructor is the facilitator of learning processes rather than an information giver. The instructor directs learners to the most useful learning resources, enriching their learning experiences. Additionally, learners are permitted opportunities to assume leadership for their learning in larger online learning communities.

CHAPTER 7

E-CoP

Communities of practice (CoPs) are groups of people who share similar goals, interests, and practices, and in doing so, employ common practices, work with the same tools, and express themselves in a common language. Through such common activity, they come to hold similar beliefs and value systems. This concept is commonly adopted in organization learning; however, it has good value in academic learning as well, such as a CoP for college advisors and advisees, teaching interest community for the instructor, and school interest groups, etc. Therefore, this chapter is designed for building online CoPs that go beyond classroom learning. Traditionally, a CoP is implemented in face-to-face environments. With availabilities of advanced communication-mediated communication (CMC) technologies, CoPs can be implemented via electronic communication technologies. This chapter suggests three designs for effective planning and managing strategies for building, fostering, and sustaining e-CoPs for organizational learning and training. While the application is broad, within the academic community, CoPs can be established within and across disciplines, perhaps initiated during a course that uses CoPs as outlined in this text, and then continued beyond the time boundaries of the course. Or, if there are existing CoPs that would be of interest to the learners in a given course setting, the instructor could refer to them, either in conjunction with a specific topic or as part of one the tasks in a design.

CoP has not reached wide acceptance in education because educators may have misunderstood its meaning. In fact, many educators have thought they were applying it because any classroom exemplifies CoP. This misconception exists because a classroom community is formed through a more formal relationship and generally it has a fixed agenda for the learning community.

Tu and McIsaac's article (2001) exemplified an effective use of CoP in an educational institution, where they formed a doctoral student CoP outside of the classroom. The faculty facilitates a common place for doctoral students, who have similar interests, to exchange their research ideas and support each other in the preparation and writing of their dissertations.

Designs introduced in this chapter are infused with two theoretical frameworks, CoP and the e-learning community. Readers can adopt all the strategies; however, since CoP is organic, it is recommended that they be applied with flexibility. The strategies and support for communities should be adjusted when they begin to grow and thrive.

DESIGN 9 BUILDING A CoP

Specifics

What	People who share similar goals, interests, and practices, and in doing so employ common practices
Who	Community members and leaders
When	Throughout entire learners' learning processes
How	Invite guest moderators
Technology	E-mail, Listserv, threaded discussions, real-time chat, audio/video conferencing systems, face-to-face
Duration	Throughout entire learners' learning processes
Grade	No grade necessary; however, rewards and encouragement may be provided.

Task 1: Identify Existing CoP

The first step is to identify existing CoPs that will enhance the organization's strategic capabilities. Many CoPs may exist in the organization because they may occur naturally in learning and/or working environments. Rather than creating them anew, find the organic CoPs, authorize them, and allow them to share knowledge and enhance their learning. Imposing organizational values onto existing CoPs by creating new ones can be extremely difficult. Identifying existing communities and allowing the community's values to emerge are critical to initiating CoPs. This is an example of when organizational culture shapes the organization and engenders organization knowledge.

Task 2: Leaders

A well-respected leader should coordinate each community. This leader is a key player who possesses important specialized knowledge, is well-connected with community members, and has heartfelt interests in community topics and knowledge. This person can be a senior practitioner, but not a renowned, world-class expert. Such an individual may impede participation by other community members because they may be intimidated by his/her reputation. After identifying a leader, the organization should devote time and authority to the leader. The leader's position can be full-time but should occupy but no less than 25 percent of their on job time. Coordinating the community can be time-consuming; therefore, the leader must have the time necessary to interact with the members of the community on a personal level. Generally, the responsibilities of the leader are to hold community members together, to keep members informed about each other's activities, to encourage interest by evolving community topics, to create opportunities for members to interact, to share ideas, insights, etc. A community based in an educational institution can have the instructor serve as leader; but having a student serve as the leader can be more effective.

Task 3: Select Topics

The topics are critical to CoPs. Frequently, organizations ask employees to share and store the wide range of information that they project, resulting in the collection and storage of a large volume of underutilized information and documents. Allowing CoPs to develop the topics they appreciate as important based on their interests can prevent this situation. The community topics should be organized to reflect "pulling" from community members (receiving assets) rather than "pushing" information out to them (providing assets). If members feel personally passionate about the work, important topics emerge easily. It is more like gardening: Seeds are planted, nurtured, and given time to grow, and seedlings cannot be encouraged to grow by pulling on their tender sprouts.

Task 4: Time to Engage

Organizations must provide generous support for an evolving CoP, if they are to receive value from the resulting learning and knowledge sharing. CoPs take time to develop and grow; therefore, community members must be given enough time to encourage their participation in community activities. This allows community members to think through the implications of other members' ideas. Time is particularly critical in asynchronous communication because it takes longer to deliver information between/among community members.

The time given to the community can be used for attending, physically and electronically, community meetings, participating and organizing a community bulletin board, developing and maintaining a community knowledge repository, etc. The time allocated should be adequate to perform team responsibilities and the time, effort, and energy expended in community activities should be valued as a part of the member's performance assessment.

Task 5: Physical Meeting

It may sound ironic that germinal e-CoPs would need physical meetings. A physical meeting is advantageous for an e-CoP if opportunities are available. Frequently, organizations host annual meetings for their employees and these are opportune times to arrange physical meetings for CoPs and e-CoPs. Physical meetings are important to energize the community because virtual communication may not be enough to build a sense of commonality, encourage enthusiasm, and establish trust. This is particularly important when the community members are located at great distances from each other.

Task 6: Online Meeting Events

The usual community activities of exchanging ideas and sharing knowledge can be supplemented by special online events. A world-renowned leader in an area of interest shared by the members can be invited by the community leader to join an online discussion or make a presentation as a guest speaker. Online discussion methods used with the invited experts can be free discussions, question-and-answer sessions, expert online presentations, interviews, panel discussions (multiple experts), etc. Tu and Corry (2003) suggested a few effective asynchronous online discussion methods that can be applied to engage CoP members in active exchanges of information and insight, read and respond, scenarios, controversies, search and critique, case study, debate, interview, panel discussions, role play, and publishing and defense.

Task 7: Evaluation

Nontraditional methods of evaluating the values of CoPs are more appropriate than traditional methods; since CoPs are organic and spontaneous, traditional evaluations won't be able to capture the dynamic creation of knowledge. The best way for the organizations to assess the value of CoPs is by listening to members' stories, which can clarify the complex relationships among activities, knowledge, and performance. The leaders should systematically gather evidence that captures the dynamic diversity and range of activities to which CoPs have evolved and in which they are involved. Additionally, the leaders can talk to members to collect stories and publish them in organization publications, such as organizational newsletters, reports, etc.

Task 8: Technology

Technological designs exert a strong influence on CoPs. The informal nature of communities and the possibilities of modern technology make the formation of communities easier to accomplish. Electronic technology can help professionals sustain and deepen relationships that they initiate through more conventional channels. The organization must provide an infrastructure that will support such communities and enable them to effectively apply their expertise.

Several guidelines can be utilized to foster CoP growth and development, using CMC technologies:

1. Facilitate and publicize discourse: Maximize and publicize electronic communication, such as e-mail lists, community Web pages, online phone lists, online threaded discussion boards, real-time discussion, and other varieties of communication.

2. Seek active support from one or more CoPs when using CMC forms: The "water-cooler" type of CoPs using a particular CMC form will increase the likelihood of a successful sharing of information.

3. Apply agent technology to prevent members from being overwhelmed by information and to allow ready access to more relevant messages; portal technology could be used to support the application cognitive (content) and social (rating) systems of intelligent agents to filter information.

The application of technology to the communities should facilitate the connection of community members and allow them to contribute information and use information in the community's knowledge base. Sense of community in a face-to-face CoP is easy to maintain because community members can walk down to the hall to talk to other community members and for online communities it is critical to keep technology accessibility easy and convenient for the members.

Task 9: Forum

Electronic communication forums are the most popular and useful technologies to support community communication and knowledge exchange. Online threaded discussions are the most common technology employed. Each community should have at least one forum to support community discourses. Frequently, sub-forums can be created to allow community members to form subgroups to exchange more specific information about a topic in privacy.

DESIGN 10 ELECTRONIC MEDIA FOR CoP

Specifics

What	Applying electronic technologies to support and foster CoP
Who	Instructor
When	Throughout learner's entire learning processes

How	Select appropriate technologies; set up the technologies
Technology	Knowledge management systems; e-Agent; soft technologies; integrate soft technologies
Duration	Throughout entire learners' learning processes
Grade	No assigned grade is necessary.

Electronic media make information and communication possible between/among community members located in different time zones and different places. These media include community Web pages, electronic member directory, listserv, knowledge management system (KMS), electronic agent (e-Agent), etc.

Task 1: Web Pages

Web pages can serve as a virtual common space for community members to visit and contribute and share information. Several online community technologies are available at Yahoo's Group (http://groups.yahoo.com) and MSN's Groups (http://groups.msn.com).

Task 2: Electronic Member Directory

The community electronic member directory should list the community members' e-mail, phone numbers, interests, personal Web page, and other personal information.

Task 3: Listservs

Listserv is a technology that is frequently forgotten. It can be applied with effective strategies to allow community members to determine how and when they would like to communicate and to be reached. Listserv doesn't need be just one-way communication, pushing information to the listserv recipients. The listserv should be set up with some options that allow listserv subscribers to determine how and when they would like to receive the listserv messages. Subscribers should be allowed to determine whether they would like the listserv messages to go to their e-mail account when a listserv message is posted. A weekly listserv can be applied that distributes listserv messages weekly. This is particularly useful for extremely active listservs that generate many messages. A listserv digest sends out a summary message regularly to the subscribers with a summary of each message posted on the listserv. This feature gives subscribers a good overview of the messages posted on the listserv and the subscribers can then determine which messages they wish to read. Some listservs also have a feature that keeps all messages posted on the listserv archive; therefore, subscribers have an opportunity to visit this archive to retrieve the missing messages, etc. Listservs also have a feature that allows subscribers to stop receiving listserv messages temporarily and it can be resumed at the subscribers' continuance. This is particularly useful when subscribers will be off e-mail for a longer period of time; therefore, listserv messages would not cause any e-mail account quota problems.

Task 4: Knowledge Management Systems

A knowledge management system (KMS) is a computer application that is capable of capturing the knowledge generated, depositing it to memory, and allowing the retrieval and presentation in an agreed upon form. Naturally, healthy CoPs generate a tremendous amount of knowledge and information for storage and revision. This information and knowledge would lack organization without a KMS. A KMS allows communities to learn while individual community members are learning; retains the knowledge generated by departed members; and provides a repository to indoctrinate new members.

Strategy 1: Identify Cultures of the Organizations

The culture of the organization must be considered when these systems are applied to enhance community learning. Organization culture shapes organization knowledge, not the KMS, and when the KMS fails to process organization knowledge, organization culture is considered to be the problem. Organization culture is difficult to change; therefore, a KMS that is designed and cultivated to fit the organization culture is more likely to be effective than attempting to reshape organization culture to fit the KMS. In an academic setting, for example, it will be much easier to establish a CoP for learners from a single discipline.

Strategy 2: KMS Architecture

The architecture of the KMS determines who has the right to design and contribute to the KMS, how knowledge should be stored, how knowledge should be retrieved, and how the knowledge should be presented after being retrieved. Community members should be granted the ownership of the KMS; therefore, the community members rather than the organization should determine the knowledge structure and leadership.

Strategy 3: Determine Taxonomy

The taxonomy of knowledge is the heart of KMS architecture. An ideal taxonomy should be intuitive for the community members because they are the owners and the users. In other words, it should reflect how community members naturally think about their knowledge domain. For instance, some communities may naturally think in numbers while some think in graphical terms.

Strategy 4: What to Capture and Store?

What to capture and store? Generally, everything processed in the community should be captured and stored in a retrievable form, such as digital documents, online forums, communication messages, etc. However, a community KMS is not a file dumping ground. The community leader or members should assume leadership responsibility to structure, design, and organize ideas that have been processed based on the community members' thinking styles.

Task 5: e-Agent

An electronic agent (e-Agent) is needed to assist community members to master the ideas exchanged in the community, particularly when it is actively exchanging large amounts of knowledge and information. It is not uncommon for members of a community to belong to multiple CoPs in an educational institution. This situation may create a negative impact on the participation of community members because an overwhelming amount of information and knowledge is generated, which may be resolved by an e-Agent. Portal technology is one of the most familiar examples of an effective e-Agent. Other examples include technologies such as an automatic scaffolding feedback system to guide learning. This is particular important in math and science education (Roschelle, Penuel, & Abrahamson, 2004). Another similar example is in students' Web searching and browsing on the Internet. While students are searching by keywords and browse the relevant Web sites, the e-Agent remembers and learns from students' learning process and recommends potential available information resources in the future.

A good portal technology has two major characteristics: centralizing and customizing. The portal gathers relevant information and knowledge based on the individual member's inquiry and presents the results in a customized format. In other words, the members are empowered to determine what, when, and how the knowledge is to be presented to them. The function of the portal technology is to enable the community member as the center of his or her own learning. It prevents the community members from being overwhelmed by the amount of information exchanged in the communities. The best example of the portal technology is My Yahoo (http://my.yahoo.com).

Task 6: Beyond Hard Technology

Generating social interaction is the key to uniting community members and advancing the formation of CoPs. Members will not commit themselves to the work of the community if they don't feel personally connected to the group's area of expertise and interest once it has been defined. Electronic communication technologies are able to deliver social interactions and are, therefore, a viable means to foster and nurture e-CoPs. Providing hard technologies, such as an electronic forum and KMSs, is not enough to generate ideal social interaction within CoPs. Frankly, ideal social interaction relies upon soft technologies, such as engaging positive social relationships and deepening trust between/ among community members. If trust and mutual recognition of competence are not developed over time, the development of CoPs may be inhibited. The next design, Social Relationship for CoP, will infuse hard and soft technologies effectively to build e-CoPs.

DESIGN 11 SOCIAL RELATIONSHIP FOR CoP

Specifics

What	Building positive social relationships
Who	Instructor, community leaders
When	Throughout entire learners' learning processes
How	Invite guest moderators
Technology	E-mail; threaded discussion board, real-time chat
Duration	Throughout entire learners' learning processes
Grade	No assigned grade is necessary.

Knowledge requires a human relationship to think about, understand, and share (McDermott, 1998). Two types of social relationships, affection and information, have been identified with positive impact on community building (Tu, 2004). The affection social relationship is the generation of a feeling that the correspondent finds you likable, and you feel affection for this person and enjoy being with them. The information relationship is centered on an information giving-receiving format in community communications. The leader is the key player in building positive social relationships. A successful leader should spend time with the community members outside of the formal meetings and online forums. He/she should contact each member regularly to demonstrate care and find out what he or she is working on and how he or she is progressing. If necessary, the leaders can refer or introduce them to other community members or other CoPs.

Task 1: Fusing Role

The leader plays an important role in fusing community members and catalyzing relationships. With this type of nurturing from the leader, community members should bring new ideas to the community and find opportunities to improve and enhance their practices. Leaders keep the community energy up by building strong affective and informative relationships among community members. When the relationships between/among members are appropriately encouraged, even when the community's topic is very scientific or theoretical, it is the human connection that builds the foundation for effective knowledge sharing.

Task 2: Trust

Employees work together, spend time together, train together, and stay together long enough certainly to provide good conditions for building CoPs but mutual trust among members is necessary to sustain them. In order to generate useful ideas and to learn from each other, the community members must be able to trust each other enough to ask for help and share ideas in formulation.

Trust will occur when members are able to master multiple online communication channels. People are accustomed to using multiple channels to get to know someone, e.g., audio and visual channels that are not present in the text-based CMC environment. More time is required for the members to become acquainted and to develop a trusting relationship and thus, an intimate social relationship. People, naturally, refuse to share ideas and personal information with others before a relationship of trust is established. Establishing self-introduction techniques and encouraging members to open themselves to others provides them with useful information. The community leaders must initiate this openness by sharing personal information with others. This openness is critically important when community members do not have any opportunity to meet face-to-face. When trust is established, community members are more assured about what roles they are supposed to play and what scripts are appropriate to (Scott & Lyman, 1968) prevent misunderstanding and misinterpretation of each other's messages. It is recommended that one should clarify any unclear or unsure message before making a judgment.

Conversing in small groups is helpful in establishing trust relationships. An effective strategy is to ask three or four community members who may have similar work practice in the organization to form a subgroup in the community. The leader can participate in these subgroups occasionally. After a few rounds of subgroup discussions that increase the trust level, the community members will establish trust with their small-group members and will be comfortable to talk more openly.

Task 3: Lurkers

Lurkers are fairly common in any online community but they do not help build a community. Generally, the lurkers obtain values without participating in the community discussion. They just want to learn who is working on what and know the field and may make contact later. It is the community leader's responsibility to engage lurkers in actively exchanging ideas. Frankly, the lurkers cannot be considered community members since they have a different agenda and take from the community without sharing. Confidentiality is in question when the communities have more lurkers participating regularly than actual community members.

Task 4: Reminders

The community of practices is an information structure in an organization. It is organic, spontaneous, and informal; therefore, it needs to be nurtured to achieve healthy growth. CoPs differ from organizational teamwork in that the organization does not exert direct control over them. Appropriate support is critical; too much support and members may lose interest; too little support and they may die. Many organizations find the decision to establish a CoP difficult because they are unable to visualize how this sort of community will benefit the organization. However, if the organization understands how CoPs work and value the contributions made by the community, the questions about profitability will be laid to rest.

REFLECTIONS

Electronic technologies enable CoP members to maximize the exchange of ideas and insight. When the organizations value CoPs and determine to apply electronic technologies to support them, both hard technologies and soft technologies must be implemented to build and nurture healthy CoPs. Simply providing hard technologies does not result in healthy communities. In fact, soft technologies inspire community members and enable them to grow and share. In other words, developing CoPs is closer to husbandry than architecture.

CHAPTER 8

Technology

Tools are required to accomplish the building of an online learning community. Online technologies function as useful tools and allow the instructor to create, foster, and sustain healthy and effective learning communities. However, simply adopting online technologies for online learning does not result in effective and healthy learning communities. It is critical to select appropriate technologies based on the different instructional needs, online circumstances, learners' capabilities, etc. The online technologies in this chapter cover three designs, Communication Technology, Collaboration Technologies, and Selecting Appropriate Online Communication, to support and enhance performance while building an online learning community.

It is more effective to make all of the multiple communication technologies available in the online learning environment to all online learners. Learners exhibit different communication styles in different places, at different times, and in different situations, making it advisable to permit them to select the communication technology with which they are most comfortable. The instructor should permit learners some laterality in determining what communication forms are used for class activities and team activities. The most frequently used technologies are threaded discussion board, real-time chat, and e-mail. However, one should not forget that other technologies are also available, such as listserv, listserv digest, video-conferencing and audio-conferencing technologies, courseware package, knowledge management systems, file management systems, and portal technologies. It is hard to distinguish communication technology from collaboration technologies because some collaboration technologies have communication functions as well.

DESIGN 12 COMMUNICATION TECHNOLOGY

Specifics

What	Know which communication technologies are available
Who	Instructor
When	Before the course begins
How	Investigate different communication technologies and be aware of their strengths and weaknesses
Technology	E-mail; threaded discussion board; real-time chat; listserv; audio/video conferencing systems; courseware packages
Duration	Variable
Grade	N/A

Online communication is center stage for online team activities; therefore, availability of effective communication technologies is critical for all online learners. Communication styles are individual for each learner and team and may change depending upon time, place, and situation. Therefore, it is advisable to provide a number of communication technologies to increase the comfort level of the learners and encourage greater involvement. This permits learners to communicate by using technologies with which they are more comfortable, thereby reducing the possibility of miscommunication. These online communication technologies fall into two major categories: asynchronous communication technologies, such as e-mail, threaded discussion board, listserv, and synchronous, such as real-time chat, audio conferencing, video conferencing, and others.

Task 1: E-mail

E-mail is the most common online communication technology because its of unique characteristics: asynchronies, personalized, availability, ease of use, low/no cost, etc. All online learners must have a "reliable" e-mail account for the class communications. Learners may have multiple e-mail accounts for different uses, but the instructor must require learners to use one of their most reliable e-mail accounts, one that they will check on a regular basis. Frequently, people who have multiple e-mail accounts do not review their e-mail on regular basis and never review their e-mail messages in some e-mail accounts. The instructor should require that each learner use a reliable e-mail account as communication technology for the class with an alternative e-mail account should the primary account fail. Learners will be out of contact if their primary e-mail server fails, stressing the advantage of alternative e-mail accounts.

Tip: School or Institutional E-Mail Account

If the school or the institution provides learners with e-mail space and access. The instructor should require that all learners use this institutional e-mail account. If the institutional e-mail server is down, all class members will have the same access problem. Then the instructor can make necessary justification for class progress. Frequently, learners use free commercial e-mail accounts for the online classes, such as hotmail and yahoo, making it more difficult to manage online class communication since the instructor does not have control on these commercial e-mail accounts.

Task 2: Exchanging Telephone Numbers and Mailing Addresses

The instructor may consider asking the learners to exchange their telephone numbers and mailing addresses. It sounds ironic that an online class asks learners to exchange nonelectronic communication information. There is nothing wrong with this. The goal of an online learning community is to achieve effective online learning. In terms of what communication technologies that online class should adopt is not limited solely to electronic technologies. This is particularly important when on-campus students are taking online courses and need to contact classmates, allowing learners opportunities to apply traditional communication methods to complete their collaborative tasks. It is, of course, impractical when learners are off-campus, live in different time zones, or live in different countries.

Task 3: Public Asynchronous Technologies

Two additional asynchronous technologies are useful for communication among and between learners—the threaded discussion board and listserv. Both are public asynchronous communication technologies and are, therefore, less private, but they are able to reach large groups of learners. The major differences between threaded discussions and listserv are that threaded discussions require learners to visit the threaded discussion board to receive and send messages, whereas listserv forwards the messages to the learners' e-mail accounts. Since most learners check their e-mail regularly, it is likely that learners will read and return listserv messages. Listserv can be an effective online communication tool, when it becomes active.

Tips

Apply the features of a weekly journal or digest offered by some listserv providers; this permits listserv recipients options on how they would like to be reached. Check with your listserv administrators for these features.

Task 4: Real-Time Chat

Real-time chat is considered an effective online communication tool because its synchronicity is similar to face-to-face conversation. Frequently, learners feel that real-time discussions allow them to communicate online without delay, more like oral communication. The instructor should be aware of some of the disadvantages encountered in real-time chat. Since it is synchronous, learners are required to be competent with keyboarding skills. Learners who lack keyboarding skills may find it difficult to maintain the tempo required to communicate in real-time. Real-time chatting is very confusing and frustrating when there are more than three people communicating. Learners may lose the sense of who is talking to whom about what. Caution must be taken when adopting real-time chat as a communication method.

Task 5: Video/Audio Conferencing

Online video and audio (AV) conferencing systems are computer-mediated communication technologies that go beyond the text-based tools. Learners are able to communicate with audio and/or visual sensory stimulation synchronously or asynchronously. AV conferencing system is considered to be the closest to face-to-face communication of any online communication tool. Although an AV conferencing system is similar to the face-to-face communication, an AV conferencing system requires large online bandwidths and large computer memory storage capacities. If these capabilities are lacking, the learners may suffer from communication difficulties and frustration because the interaction is likely not to proceed smoothly.

Task 6: Availability

We have discussed several online communication technologies that can be useful for communication for learners. How do we obtain these technologies? Many schools have offered courseware packages to their faculty to support online teaching. The courseware includes BlackBoard, WebCT, FirstClass, etc. Additionally, there are a few commercial communication technologies that are free to use, such as Microsoft, Yahoo, Hotmail, Microsoft NetMeeting, etc.

It is more effective to make all of the multiple communication technologies available to online learners. Learners exhibit different communication styles in different places, at different times, and in different situations, making it advisable to permit them to select the communication technology with which they are most comfortable. The instructor should permit learners some laterality in determining what communication forms are used for class activities and team activities. The most frequently used technologies are threaded discussion board, real-time chat, and e-mail. However, other technologies are also available, such as listserv, listserv digest, video-conferencing, and audio-conferencing.

Tip

Should I use all communication technologies in my online learning community?

The answer is "No." However, it is important to provide learners and their teams with a wide selection of online communication technologies. In fact, it is rare that one course requires that learners process all of the different types of communication technologies. Learners may adopt different communication technologies for their team communications; therefore, the instructor should make these technologies available and accessible for them, allowing learners to select the best fit of communication technologies for their team while building an effective learning community. If there is the need to designate a certain communication technology for required tasks, the instructor should evaluate the learners accessibility to the technology, the learners' hardware capacity, the learners' ability to mange the technology, etc.

DESIGN 13 COLLABORATION TOOLS

Specifics

What	Knowing availabilities of online collaboration technologies
Who	Instructor
When	Before the course begins
How	Investigate different online collaboration technologies
Technology	Virtual common place; file management systems; online database; portal technologies
Duration	Varies
Grade	No grade assignment is necessary.

Effective tools must be identified that support collaboration in addition to communication tools to assist learners and teams to organize the large amounts of information exchanged during team collaboration. Simple e-mail exchanges among team members may work most times, but when more interaction is generated among team members, more effective and powerful collaboration tools should be provided by the class, file exchanging, sharing technology, etc. Commonly, information-exchanging processes are not captured and retained; therefore, applying effective collaboration tools to support file sharing, resource sharing, management, etc., is important. These collaboration tools include advanced online database tools, spreadsheets, file managing systems, portal technology, etc. These tools are important to accomplish the necessary knowledge and information-sharing functions.

Task 1: Virtual Common Place

Each team should have a common place of its own online for communication. This space should be designated only for the team members and the instructor. This online space should be separated from the class common space. Members of other teams should not have access to this team common place unless the team is willing to share their communication with other teams.

This common place should include a few useful technologies to assist teams to manage their team tasks, such as team announcement, team discussion, team Cyber Café, team Chat Corner, and team calendar. A team announcement will allow team members to make any general announcement to the team members. Team discussion applies threaded discussion technology to allow team members to discuss their team business and tasks asynchronously, while a team Cyber Café provides the team members a place to carry on social conversations, to build social relationships, and to improve team *espirit de corps*. Since asynchronous technology takes longer to accomplish communication goals, team Chat Corner, a real-time discussion technology, should be provided to support the team's discussions. With the use of both synchronous and asynchronous technologies, teams are equipped with a wide-range of collaboration tools. Teams can select the most appropriate technologies to conduct collaborative work.

Currently, most courseware packages provide team space tools that allow teams to manage their team tasks, BlackBoard, WebCT, FirstClass, etc. These courseware packages provide features that support team management; the instructors do not need to create them from scratch. If the courseware is not available for the class, the instructor can suggest that teams can take advantage of the commercial online community tool, such as MSN's Groups (http://groups.msn.com) or Yahoo's Groups (http:// groups.yahoo.com) etc. These online spaces are generally free. The disadvantage is that these free services generally will have pop-out or flashing ads while using these services.

Task 2: File Managing System

Frequently, team members need to share and exchange their files in addition to communications. Certainly, e-mail systems for exchanging and sharing files is appropriate; however, file sizes that are larger than the

Figure 8.1
The Advantages and Disadvantages of File Management Systems

	E-mail	Threaded Discussion Board	FTP	Drop Box
Ease of use	Very easy	Very easy	May require some knowledge	Easy
Additional application required	No. Learners should have their e-mail applications.	No	Yes. Learners must have FTP application installed on their workstations.	Generally no
Large file size	E-mail account quota limitation	Generally not	Generally not	Generally not
Ease of setup	Yes	Available in courseware packages	Require knowledge in FTP	Available in courseware packages
Override files	Less likely	Less likely	Yes	Less likely
Archive	Weak	Fair	Good	Strong
Risk of virus	There is potential that a virus may infect the e-mail account and learners' workstations	Generally there is no concern of viruses unless learners download the infected files onto their work-stations. Potentially, the infected files may cause problems on the server. It requires the server to have robust virus filtering functions	Same as the threaded discussion board	Same as the threaded discussion board

e-mail account space limitation may create some frustration and technical difficulties for the teams, requiring time-consuming gyrations to retrieve e-mails. Teams should be given a file sharing and exchanging system to manage team files to facilitate their collaborative learning. This system provides a common place for team members to exchange and share files in a more public online space that functions as a depository or archive. Such a facility will eliminate the disadvantages of using e-mail to exchange and share files. For example, if team members lose their files in e-mail on their computers, there are no backup files. Teams can also use the file management system to manage their team work files, such as the team goals, the team policy and procedures, team project files, etc. Since these files are kept in the team public area, each individual team member will have equal access to the files, and the potential to modify or update the files.

The simplest technology that can be applied is a threaded discussion board. Commonly, threaded discussion boards come with an attachment feature that allows users to attach one or more files to the threaded discussion messages.

FTP (File Transfer Protocol) is another tool that can be used as a file management system. The instructor can create an FTP account for each team to upload and download the team files.

Digital Drop Box is an extension of FTP. Basically, Digital Drop Box works like FTP; however, it provides a more user-friendly interface to upload and download files. Unlike FTP, it doesn't require additional applications to upload and download files. Generally, Digital Drop Box has more advanced features for organizing uploaded files, such as sorting, time stamps, displaying file property information, etc. The team space created in the courseware packages generally provides this tool for exchanging and sharing files.

Task 3: Database-Driven System

An online database can serve as a depository to capture and store knowledge. It also features input and retrieval functions that support learning. Since a database is not static storage, learners must play active roles in obtaining necessary knowledge and information. Learners must utilize critical thinking skills when they conduct a database search (query); otherwise, relevant information and knowledge will not be retrieved. This process allows learners to process deeper learning rather than simply being fed information. Second, learners should have opportunities to make contributions to the database, facilitating the accumulation of information and knowledge from multiple sources rather than the distillation of information from a single source. This promotes social learning by providing multiple perspectives on gathered information. Through these basic information-processing procedures, learning processes are advanced to a higher level.

Frequently, teams will share resources and information during the team work process. A powerful tool is needed to organize these valuable resources and information. Applying database technology to organize the resources and information is useful. The most common phenomenon in online learning is sharing online resources with others. Commonly, learners use e-mail, listserv, threaded discussion board, and real-time chat technologies to share online resources. These technologies, except the threaded discussion board, have one drawback and that is archiving. In other words, if learners do not archive the online resources, it will be difficult to relocate and retrieve them. Even when learners archive the exchange resources, it is still challenging to search and retrieve them.

Database technology has the potential to manage and improve the resource exchanges within the teams. Additionally, it can be married with online technology and be made available online. The basic mechanism of the online database allows learners to make contributions to the database, edit/update the resources, search the database, and customize the display of the search results. These features support and enhance the learner-centered instruction design because learners are engaged in contributing their knowledge to the database, to obtain new knowledge; learners need to search the database to retrieve the deposited knowledge. The research results are displayed in a customized form that supports learners' learning styles. Since everyone has equal access to the database, the database is a dynamic knowledge depository and search results will be varied from learners' different cognitive search (keywords).

A database-driven system is a powerful tool to manage the exchange and sharing of knowledge accumulated in an online learning community; however, it requires more advanced technology design skills to accomplish. Generally, a database system is not available in any courseware package or any free commercial online space. Available database technologies are: Microsoft Access (http://www.msn.com/access), and FileMaker Pro (http://www.filemakerpro.com), both commercial; and mySequel, available as Open Source Software. There are many more, of course.

Task 4: Portal Technology

Portal technology is an important tool to enhance online collaborative learning. A portal is an entry point to resources on the World Wide Web. Generally, portal software will contain online search engines, links to useful pages, news, etc. Advanced portals may provide customized information to suit the needs of online users. Learners can utilize advanced portals to tailor their inquiries with the exact information they require rather than the plethora of information that is received without their assistance.

Learners and teams are granted many powerful tools to enhance their collaborative learning community. To access each individual tool, learners are required to visit each tool separately. This may result in an overwhelming challenge to access different collaboration tools. A portal technology may offer a centralized location (a Web page) that directs learners to different tools rather than all of the tools being scattered. This is particularly useful when the team sizes are large and there is active interaction in teams. Generally, courseware packages offer some features of team portal functions while online commercial space offers powerful online portal technology for their online community space. Creating portals specific to a course remains a challenge with today's technology.

Tips

Portal technology can be implemented via database technology. More advanced skills are required to design a portal powered by a database. The suggestion is that one should check with their Web master, network administrator, or technical support staff at their institution.

DESIGN 14 SELECTING APPROPRIATE ONLINE COMMUNICATION

Specifics

What	Select appropriate and effective communication technologies to enhance learning
Who	Instructor
When	Before the course
How	Select, analyze, and devise effective communication technologies
Technology	All communication technologies
Duration	Vary
Grade	NA

Selecting appropriate CMC technologies and applying them to the online learning environment is a very important process. Currently, there are a variety of technologies available, such as e-mail, threaded discussion board, real-time chat, listserv, video/audio conferencing, MOOs (Multiple, Object Oriented), and MUDs (Multi-User Dungeon). However, not all of them need to be adopted into the curriculum. In fact, it is rare for one to be able to incorporate all CMC technologies. Each CMC form possesses different inherent attributes that may shape users' online interaction. Here are strategies to follow:

Task 1: Ensuring Keyboarding Skills and Accuracy

Many users are not good at keyboarding, particularly users who have English as Second Language (ESL), when English is the language used in the online learning. One should be aware of each individual's keyboarding skills and accuracy. It may be necessary to provide training and time allotted for practice. Voice recognition is a useful tool to replace keyboarding. Several versions of voice recognition software are available: IBM Via Voice (http://www-306.ibm.com/software/voice/viavoice/index.shtml), and Dragon Naturally Speaking (http://www.scansoft.com/naturallyspeaking/). Asynchronous communication technologies can be applied, such as e-mail, threaded discussion board, listserv, etc., to allow the user more time to generate thoughts and respond to communications.

Task 2: Using Appropriate Communication Channels

Each CMC form provides a different communication channel. Generally they are leaner than face-to-face communication. Text-based communication generally provides less social context cues, whereas video/audio conferencing provide more. The users' characteristics determine the most suitable form to integrate into the learning environment. These two continuums provide the relations of different CMC forms in social context cues and time dependence. More context cues and more response time are not necessarily better for users. The situation and the characteristics of users and context determine when to use what technologies.

Figure 8.2
The Continuum of Relation of CMC Forms and Social Context Cues

Less context cues   More context cues

◄──►

[Threaded discussion   [E-   [Listserv]   [Real-time   [MOOs/   [Video/audio
board]   mail]   chat]   MUDs]   conferencing]

Figure 8.3
The Continuum of Relation of CMC Forms and Response Time

Less response time   More response time

◄──►

[Video/audio   [MOOs/   [Real-time   [Listserv]   [E-   [Threaded discussion
conferencing]   MUDs]   chat]   mail]   board]

Task 3: Using Emoticons and Paralanguage

Emoticons and paralanguage gives more emotional feeling to online users. It compensates for the absence of social context cues. Using emoticons ("☺," "☻," "<G>" etc.) and paralanguage (acronyms, abbreviations, all caps, exclaim, slang, colors, colloquialism, etc.) is highly recommended. More information on emoticons and paralanguage can be found on the Smiley Dictionary (http://www.smileydictionary.com/).

Task 4: Following Multi-Threaded Discussions

Users sometimes have difficulty determining "who" is talking to "whom" about "what" in a multi-threaded discussion environment. Two strategies are suggested.

Strategy 1: Using Strategic Snipping

It is useful to use strategic snipping to simulate conversational overlaps: restate or quote previous message prior expressing one's thoughts. Ex: John said: "Computer technology should be used as tools." Basically I agree with. . . .

Strategy 2: Using Formulations and Index Repairs

Using formulations and index repairs to emulate conversational practice: identify which message, what part of message first, and then continue one's thoughts. Ex: In Mary's posting on April 15, she discussed social learning theory. . . .

REFLECTIONS

Technology is a tool to enhance learners' learning. The attributes of technologies influence learners' applications of technologies. It is important to understand technologies' strengths and weaknesses to enable the instructor to provide effective and appropriate strategies for learners in technology-based communication and collaboration. For example, e-mail has been perceived as a "casual written communication" method. Frequently, we see e-mail messages composed using formal language that increases the psychological distance. In other words, the issues of applying technology for communication and collaboration are not only which technologies we use, but also how we use them.

CHAPTER 9

Social Collegial

Active online social interaction has been one of the most desirable learning situations. "No interaction, no learning" (Gunawardena, 1995). Online communication and interaction are different from traditional encounters because of the lean channels of online communications. It is text-based and it lacks social context cues, etc. Therefore, computer-mediated communication (CMC) requires different communication styles and strategies. In fact, "Do we know how to speak online?" is an important question that has been raised in recent studies (Tu, 1999). The answer is, "not quite," because many people have felt that CMC is cold, impersonal, unsociable, and insensitive. This chapter provides designs and strategies to enhance online social interaction in a learning environment. It is composed of two designs, Design 15 Understanding Social Context, and Design 16 Optimizing Online Interactivity. Useful and practical strategies for each design are discussed to provide how-to knowledge. These strategies are well thought out and organized, allowing anyone to apply them to their practice to increase the level of online interaction and learning.

DESIGN 15 UNDERSTANDING SOCIAL CONTEXT

Specifics

What   Building social collegial online community
Who   Instructor

When	Throughout the entire course
How	Knowing online participants; building positive social relationships; gain trust; apply effective technologies; grant a feeling of privacy
Technology	E-mail; threaded discussion board; real-time chat
Duration	Throughout the entire course
Grade	No assigned grade is necessary.

Social context is constructed from the CMC users' characteristics and their perception of the CMC environment. Online users form the basis of an online learning community. A better understanding of online users provides an opportunity to increase the level of online interaction and learning. Several effective tasks and strategies that enhance online interaction are outlined: familiarity with recipients, informational relationships, better trust relationships, personally informative types of social relationships, positive psychological attitude toward the technology, and privacy in access location.

Task 1: Knowing Your Online Users

The first step necessary to initiate online interaction and learning is being familiar with your correspondents. A certain level of familiarity is necessary to promote online interaction; in fact, outright conflict and flaming can easily be generated online when the participants are strangers. Self-introductions must be accompanied by follow-up communication. The self-instruction can be integrated into the beginning of the class and the team initiation. Here are the steps and strategies you should follow to get to know your online users:

Strategy 1: Start with Self-Introduction

Here are some questions that are useful for online users to know:

- Who you are?
- What do you do?
- What do you like/dislike?
- Use three things to describe yourself.
- Where are you from?
- What is your favorite food?
- What are your favorite colors?
- Why did you join this course/group?
- What is the most memorable thing that has occurred in your life?
- What do you consider to be your most important accomplishment?

Strategy 2: Follow-Up Self-Introduction Postings

After posting the first self-introduction, follow-up postings should be encouraged that expand the depth and breadth of familiarity of online users. Online participants must respond to the self-introductions that others provide. If the self-introduction does not flow well, online moderators or the instructor must generate more conversation or ask questions about the individuals and ask them to share their experiences.

Strategy 3: Maintain a Database

A permanent self-introduction database accompanied by individual pictures is very desirable for online communication. This database serves as a reference that allows the participants to review each other's backgrounds anytime they wish. Several database software packages can be used to support this step: FileMaker Pro (http://www.filemaker.com/index.html), Macromedia ColdFusion (http://www.macromedia.com/software/coldfusion/), and Microsoft Access (http://office.microsoft.com/home/office. aspx?assetid=FX01085791), etc. Streaming video/audio self-introduction is another option that one can use to enhance this process. This would add a human touch that is not available in a text-based database. Additionally, the instructor, moderators, and staff could introduce themselves through streaming media if at all possible (see Chapter 8 Technology for more details on each technology).

Task 2: Building Informal Relationships

Online interaction is lubricated by informal relationships. When a relationship is perceived as formal, less communication and interaction will occur. The instructor-learner relationship is generally considered to be more formal. Here are the steps and strategies to produce informal relationships:

Strategy 1: Use Casual Online Communication

The higher-ranking person (learners, moderators, employers, administrators) must utilize less formal conversation styles to communicate with subordinates (students, employees). Less formal communication strategies can be used:

- Use "Hi" instead of "Dear" to start the message.
- Use the person's first name, or nickname.
- Start with a warm greeting, such as "How was your weekend?" "Do you feel better?" or "It is nice to hear from you!" etc. Do not start the message with pure context.
- In the end of message, use "Regards" or "Best wishes" instead of "Sincerely yours." The signature should use first name rather than full name with rank or title, such as Ph.D., CEO, Principal, etc.

Strategy 2: Continue Informal Conversations

Informal communication styles must be used constantly to assure an ongoing relationship. Learners need more time to sense the instructor's casualness.

Task 3: Gaining Better Trust Relationships

Trust takes a longer time to develop among online users because of the lack of social context cues and physical contact in an online learning environment. A sense of antagonism can be easily generated when trust has not been well established. Here are the strategies that should be followed:

Strategy 1: Avoid Anonymity

Unless there is a good reason to use it because it creates feelings of distrust and insecurity.

Strategy 2: Be Patient

Time is required to generate a trusting relationship.

Strategy 3: Encourage Sharing Personal Information

One must encourage users to share their personal life experiences. When one is open to others, others are more likely to be open to us.

Task 4: Building Caring and Informative Social Relationships

Caring and informative types of social relationships will provide users with a more comfortable and useful social interaction. Adversely, service and status types of social relationship will degrade online interaction. Here are the strategies that can be followed:

Strategy 1: Express Personal Concerns

Use messages to express personal concerns.

Strategy 2: Show Appreciation

Always say "Thank you!" to *show appreciation* as a substitute for the smiling in a face-to-face environment.

Strategy 3: Assist and Support Others

Assist and support others with information or resources rather than just receiving information and support from others.

Task 5: Ensuring Appropriate Technology Perceptions

Many online users have had negative experiences working with technology. Do not expect that all online users have positive technology experiences. Here are strategies to follow:

Strategy 1: Understand Students' Comfort Levels Toward Technology and Their Feelings About Technology

An understanding of student feelings about technology should be developed through casual conversation.

Strategy 2: Be Patient with Users

It takes a long time to change one's feeling about technology.

Strategy 3: Be Understanding

Attempt to understand the individual's situation. Do not judge; do not castigate people for having less experience with technology, and less understanding.

Task 6: Providing More Private Locations

Computer users are more likely to communicate more freely when the computer access location is more private because they feel that the people around them cannot observe what is written on the screen and scrutinize their keyboarding skills. Users feel constrained in public computer access areas, computer labs, libraries, or when they must share computers. It is harder for them to talk freely online and share more personal information. Here are strategies to follow:

Strategy 1: Encourage Private Access Locations

Encourage users to use a place where they feel more private, more comfortable, and safer to participate in CMC.

Strategy 2: Provide Access Opportunities for Users

If possible, *provide access opportunities for users*, such as reserved rooms, and recommend access locations, etc. If the budget allows, loan laptops or desktop computers to users and allow them to access CMC from home.

Strategy 3: Be Understanding

Many users must access CMC from a public area. Long waiting lines, less privacy, less comfort, and feeling unsafe will have a negative impact upon online interaction.

DESIGN 16 OPTIMIZING ONLINE INTERACTIVITY

Specifics

What	Optimize online interactivity
Who	Learners; instructors

When	Throughout the entire course
How	Timely responses; use stylistic communication styles; adopt communication strategies; apply appropriate message lengths; select appropriate task types; apply appropriate team size
Technology	E-mail; threaded discussion board
Duration	Throughout the entire course
Grade	Varies

Task 1: Providing Timely Responses

Lack of a timely response to an asynchronous message generates a feeling of misunderstanding. This miscommunication will degrade online interaction and learning. Here are suggested strategies:

Strategy 1: One or Two Days for E-mail

It is recommended that in the e-mail setting the appropriate response time is one day for an e-mail transmitted on a weekday and two to three days for a weekend.

Strategy 2: Short Notification

If one is unable to respond within in a reasonable period of time, a short notice should be sent stating when a complete response is to be expected.

Strategy 3: Away Notification

If one will be away from e-mail contact, one should take advantage of "Vacation Automatic Notice" that will notify message senders when one will be back in e-mail contact.

Task 2: Using Stylistic Communication

Stylistic communication (Norton, 1986) is very useful. They have a positive impact on users' online interaction by affecting feelings toward others and influencing learning.

Strategy 1: Attentive

Be responsive to CMC messages.

Strategy 2: Impression-Leaving

Appreciate, and be willing and eager to answer any question.

Strategy 3: Relaxed

People feel more informal and casual.

Strategy 4: Acquiescent

One must listen (read) what others have to say and share.

Strategy 5: Friendly

Be very nice, be polite, be courteous, and use inviting speech.

Strategy 6: Open

Share personal information openly and appropriately.

Strategy 7: Animated

Use emoticons and paralanguage to express their feelings and make messages more stimulating online.

Strategy 8: Dramatic

Apply story telling, humor, puns, and double takes to enrich the conversations.

Strategy 9: Personal

Use a more inviting speaking tone, and initiate an invitation to someone for a (short) discussion or conversation.

Task 3: Adopting Communication Strategies

There are several communication strategies that should be applied to online communication. They are: initiation of conversation, greeting, praise, etc.

Strategy 1: Initiating Communication

Do not wait for others to initiate a communication. Initiating communication shows that one is willing to build a friendship as well as to share concerns. This makes people feel friendlier, more personable, and warmer.

Strategy 2: Greeting

A salutation and a complimentary close are critical components of messages that occur at the beginning and the end of each conversation. The greeting does not need to be lengthy, even a short greeting makes the CMC conversation friendlier. The message should begin by naming the others, "Hi Andy," or "Hello! Charlie." Greater formality occurs when titles and the last names are used in the greeting, as in "Dear Mr. Watson." This courtesy will identify the recipient and provide a warmer, more personal feeling. After the salutation it is good to exchange greetings that create a more personal, informal, and friendly environment and show concern for the recipient:

- "It's nice to hear from you!"
- "Thanks for writing me back!"
- "How was your weekend?"
- "Did you have a good holiday?"
- "How's your final project going?" or
- "Do you feel better?"

The complimentary closing may be preceded by benedictory remarks: "Any questions?" "Please feel free to ask me if you have more questions." "It was nice to have this discussion with you. I had a good time." "See you in the class!" or "Thanks for your time."

Strategy 3: Praise

Showing appreciation and praising others produces a conversation that is more pleasant and interactive. It can be used at any place in the message and whenever it is necessary. Some examples follow:

- "Thanks for your information!"
- "Your ideas are very interesting!"
- "I really appreciate your time and efforts."

Task 4: Using Appropriate Message Length

Message length exerts an influence on learners' interactions. Real-time discussion should have the shortest message length, followed by e-mail, and the threaded discussion board messages. Real-time discussion should be conducted like oral conversation. The sentence structure and grammar are less important. E-mail is of a moderate length. E-mail should be treated more like a *"causal written conversation."* The sentence structure and grammar should be more important than in a real-time discussion because the asynchronous characteristic makes messages more permanent; in real-time discussion the message disappears when the discussion is ended. The threaded discussion board can be conducted as more formal writing, so it tends to be longer, the writing style can be more formal, and the word choice can be less oral. Sentence structure and grammar should be more rigid since the message is permanent and public.

It is suggested that when the e-mail message is longer than usual or contains a long document, the document should be sent as an attachment; this allows the recipient to open it on a word processor and review it and answer it off-line.

Task 5: Selecting Appropriate Task Types

Task types are influenced by the online interaction of users. Several more interactive task types are: planning, creativity, intellectual discussions, decision making, and social tasks. Here are the strategies to follow:

Strategy 1: Collaborative Learning Exercise

Apply collaborative learning exercises (team project) and related Internet topics for threaded discussions.

Strategy 2: Sharing Ideas

Engaging users to share ideas and responding to others' ideas improves thinking and deepens understanding.

Strategy 3: Make Their Own Decision

Allow users to make their own decisions and provide different supporting technologies and guidelines, and then allow them to negotiate what, when, where, and how to learn.

Strategy 4: Social Activity

Provide opportunities for users to engage in social activities, such as sharing their life experiences and talking about their work, family, communities, recent personal events, etc.

Task 6: Determining Appropriate Communication Group Size

The size of the discussion group exerts a major impact on a learner's interactions, particularly in real-time discussions. It is recommended that the size of the group for real-time discussion should be limited to two or three participants if possible and no more than four. If a larger group is necessary, a strategy that provides equal turn taking must be applied. Threaded discussion boards should be limited to twelve to fifteen participants. Otherwise, participants who are unable to follow the discussion may simply give up the discussion or will skip reading many of the discussion messages.

REFLECTIONS

This chapter intends to assist in enhancing online learning through social interaction. Two practical designs, Design 15 Understanding Social Context, and Design 16 Optimizing Interactivity are discussed and different strategies are provided. The tasks and strategies should be followed as closely as possible. However, we should apply these task and strategies with realistic justification because different contexts may have different characteristics and needs. The strategies must be modified to comply with the local cultures, contexts, and characteristics.

CHAPTER 10

Assessment

DESIGN 17 COLLABORATIVE EVALUATION

Specifics

What	Team activity
Who	Learners, instructors
When	End of the team project/activity
How	Set up goals and policy; communicate the goals; evaluate; perform extended activities
Technology	E-mail, FTP, Digital Drop Box
Duration	Allowed at least 3–4 days
Grade	No additional credit assigned for participating in this evaluation. Grades for the team project are based upon the instructor, self, and peer evaluations.

Collaborative evaluation, when applied to the performance of team projects, encourages learners to assume full responsibility for their learning. This form of evaluation includes the instructor's evaluation, a self-evaluation, and a peer evaluation. The instructor will assign a percentage of the grade for the team project and the remainder, consisting of the above elements, is distributed as determined by each team. Learners are granted an opportunity to negotiate their evaluations. In other words, each teacher will provide the percentage selected by the teams.

Collaborative evaluation for online collaborative learning doesn't work if it is just simply applying these methods for the collaborative team project in online classes. It takes effective planning to accomplish ideal collaborative evaluation.

Task 1: Communicate Goals

The online collaborative evaluation should start by communicating the goals and the purposes of collaborative evaluation with learners, permitting them a good understanding of online collaborative evaluation and the instructor's expectations.

Strategy 1: Explain Importance and Rationale

The instructor should explain the importance and the rationale for this method of evaluation before adopting and applying it to the online collaborative learning.

The general goals of online collaborative evaluation are:

- Promote learner-centered learning.
- Encourage learners to be responsible for their learning.
- Learn effective collaborative learning skills.
- Advance fair evaluation for online collaborative learning projects.
- Provide active online collaboration.

The instructor should explain these general goals and any additional specific goals depending upon the contents and other circumstances.

Strategy 2: Explain Procedures

After communicating the goals, the instructor should explain the procedures of the online collaborative evaluation. It is suggested that the instructor begin by organizing grade proportions. One may ask what weights the instructor will apply to different evaluation methods. It is advisable to begin with a percentage allocation for different evaluation methods; for example, the instructor's evaluation occupies 50 percent of the score on the collaborative team project, while the other 50 percent is allocated for peer evaluation and self-evaluation. Or, the instructor retains 50 percent and the remainder is allocated for the peer/self-evaluations allowing a balance on the final grade for the team projects. In fact, the grade allocation can depend on the instructor's assessment of the maturity and experience of the learners and a more liberal amount can be given to them. In this chapter, the example of half/half is applied to explain online collaborative evaluation.

Figure 10.1
The Possible Combinations of Peer and Self-Evaluation Based
on a Three-Learner Team

Combination	Instructor (%)	Self-Evaluation (%)	Peer Evaluation 1 (%)	Peer Evaluation 2 (%)	Total (%)
1	50	20	15	15	100
2	50	30	10	10	100
3	50	40	5	5	100

Strategy 3: Negotiate Evaluations

Since half of grade is given to the peer and self-evaluation, each team should negotiate how they would like to allocate that 50 percent of the grade. Each team should be given the opportunity to determine the percentages applied to peer and self-evaluation. Any combination of percentages is appropriate, but both peer evaluation and self-evaluation must be included, regardless of the percentage allocated to each. For instance, the combination that can be allocated to peer evaluation is 45 percent, while self-evaluation receives 5 percent or simply 25 percent for both peer and self-evaluation. Figure 10.1 presents examples of possible combinations of the allocated percentages in collaborative evaluation.

Strategy 4: Devising an Evaluation Form

It is also important to share the evaluation form (see Appendix A) with the learners while communicating the goals of collaborative evaluations. The form should be deliberated upon during the course introduction and when giving descriptive feedback when grades are given. This will permit learners more options to exploit the evaluation effectively.

Task 2: Setting Team Goals and Criteria

After communicating the goals of collaborative evaluation, each team should discuss its team goals, policy, procedures, and evaluation criteria; this should occur as early as possible so each member of the team is informed. The instructor must assist each team to devise its team governance documents, including team goals, policies, procedures, and evaluation criteria. A guideline for setting team governance should be provided to assist teams to accomplish this initial task. Some tips to help learners to evaluate peers' performance may be needed (see Figure 10.2 and Figure 10.3).

Figure 10.2
Guidelines for Setting Up Team Governance

Each team should communicate and discuss team governances to prepare for their online collaborative learning project. After the teams finish all of these tasks, the teams should submit one copy of these documents to the instructor as a record. Changing or modifying the team documents is permissible if decided unanimously by all team members. A revised copy should be submitted to the instructor. These documents will not be graded.

1. Team goals
   - Read the online collaborative learning project assigned by the instructor.
   - Set up the team goals to meet the requirements of the collaborative learning project.

2. Team policy and procedure
   - Set up the necessary policies and procedures that team members can follow to accomplish the collaborative project.
   - Identify leadership if necessary.

3. Team evaluation criteria
   - Review the collaborative evaluation form provided by the instructor.
   - Review the team project requirements and discuss with team members to determine how the teams should allocate the percentage on peer and self-evaluations.
   - Example:

Combination	1	2	3
Instructor (%)	50	50	50
Self-Evaluation (%)	20	30	40
Peer Evaluation 1 (%)	15	10	5
Peer Evaluation 2 (%)	15	10	5
Total (%)	100	100	100

   - Determine the evaluation criteria, such as communication, intellectual contribution, support, leadership, etc.
   - Peer and self-evaluations should be in a descriptive form with the agreed upon percentage allocation.

4. Communication methods
   - Identify effective computer-mediated communication (CMC) technologies.
   - Exchange communication information.
     - Exchange e-mail and alternative e-mail contacts.
     - Exchange telephone number and post office mailing address if necessary.
   - Discuss how team members should communicate, as well as how frequently.

Figure 10.3
How to Evaluate Peer's Performance

The purpose of the peer evaluation is to provide appropriate feedback to assist the peer in improving individual collaborative work. Fellow team members are able to best evaluate each other because they are aware of what occurred during their team project. Therefore, please see it as a positive chance to help fellow team members. The instructor will not provide criteria for the team peer evaluations. Perhaps the team may want to decide how peers should be evaluated and determine some evaluation criteria.

In general, there are a few common areas that peers can evaluate, such as communication, intellectual contribution, support, leadership, etc.

Communication: Are peers maintaining good communication?

Intellectual contribution: Does the peer make significant intellectual contributions to the team work?

Support: Does the peer demonstrate enthusiastic support of others?

Leadership: Does the peer demonstrate leadership capabilities that inspire teamwork?

Cooperation: Does the peer demonstrate a cooperative attitude and shoulder his/her share of the team's activities?

Task 3: Final Evaluation

After the teams finish their actual online collaborative learning projects, the collaborative evaluations should take place. The collaborative evaluation form introduced at the beginning of the collaborative project will be used and submitted electronically. The form can be used for instructor, peer, and self-evaluations. The instructor will collect all of collaborative evaluation forms and consolidate the feedback and grades. It is important that the instructor should share the feedback and grades that each individual received from the instructor, peers, and themselves. Sharing the feedback with the each individual provides a good opportunity for learners to improve their collaborative learning skills. The feedback may be anonymous or open. In fact, the instructor can leave these decisions for each individual team at the beginning of collaborative learning.

Task 4: Extended Activities

An extended activity can be added to the post-collaborative evaluations by responding to the feedback that learners receive. Learners can make any necessary response, reflection, or comment on the feedback that they receive from the instructor and peers. Based on the received feedback, learners can propose strategies to improve their online collaborative learning experiences.

DESIGN 18 REFLECTIONS

Specifics

What	Learners share and reflect about their online collaborative learning experiences.
Who	Learners; instructor
When	Completion of the online collaboration or at the end of the course
How	Set up technology; determine the length and format; reflect on learning experiences; facilitate this process
Technology	Threaded discussion board; real-time chat
Duration	1–2 weeks for threaded discussions; at least one hour for real-time chat
Grade	Grades can be assigned as regular lesson discussions.

The activity of reflection on online collaborative learning community (OCLC) is an opportunity to engage learners in self-reflection on the different designs of OCLC and an opportunity to allow the instructor and instructional designers to improve their designs and implementations of OCLC. The online collaborative learning community emphasizes the learning process and the learning outcome; therefore, it is critical for learners to review and reflect on their individual engagement in OCLC, regardless of whether it was a success or failure as a learning experience. This review and reflection opportunity will assist learners to project some practical strategies for their future learning and to be equipped with better skills in OCLC. These useful and practical strategies may come from self-review and reflection, classmates' suggestions, inspirations from classmates, etc. The instructor or instructional designer can seize this opportunity to formulate ideas on how their designs can be improved upon or modified for future teaching.

Task 1: Technology

Both threaded discussions and real-time chats can be applied to implement this reflection activity. Since this is designed as an entire class discussion activity, a threaded discussion form may be more appropriate, particularly for large classes. If a real-time discussion is used, the number of class members should remain small because real-time discussions may cause confusion during the discussion with all learners talking at the same time. Turn-taking strategies should be applied and the instructor should lead and organize the discussions.

Task 2: Length of Discussions

The reflection discussions should occur during the last week of the class or later. If a threaded discussion board is used, a week should be designated. If a real-time chat is used, at least one hour should be designated.

Task 3: Discussion Format

Effective discussion questions should be composed and posted. Since reflection discussion is part of the online collaborative learning community, it is recommended that it should be made a requirement of the class; therefore, all learners have opportunities to review and reflect upon their learning process and experiences. In other words, grade points can be allocated to this activity. It may be necessary to separate each OCLC design for discussion since an online class may integrate more than one OCLC design. Here are a few good questions that can be asked for the reflection discussions:

1. Please describe how well or poorly you participated in team moderations. How will you improve or modify your participation if you have an opportunity to participate in team moderations in the future?
2. What strategies are useful when participating in an online debate? Please share them with the class.
3. Please describe your learning experiences interacting with virtual experts.
4. Did you have free riders? If yes, how did your team resolve this issue? If no, do you have any strategies to improve this situation?
5. How do you like the idea of an online collaborative evaluation?
6. What are the most challenging things in the online collaborative learning community?

Task 4: Moderation

During the reflection discussions, the instructor should scrutinize the discussions closely. It is important to ensure that all learners are able to engage in self-reflection and are able to support each other in useful strategies to improve their OCLC skills. Certainly, it is appropriate for the instructor to take on the task of moderation; however, better knowledge construction is frequently derived from peers. It is important for the instructor to guide and help learners by providing their reflections, providing learners with effective learning strategies, and enabling them to improve their learning skills continuously for the future.

REFLECTIONS

Collaborative evaluation is an effective way to improve online collaborative learning. By applying instructor evaluations, peer evaluations, self-evaluation, and self-determined evaluations, the online collaborative learning process improves the learner-centered instructional designs. Collaborative evaluations for online collaborative learning should be performed carefully. The intention is not to pass all of the learning responsibilities to the learners; instead, learners should become responsible by negotiating with their instructor and their peers. In other words, the instructor should continuously and consistently provide guidance and instruction to the learners and the teams; as a result, the learners are able to maximize their positive learning experiences.

PART III

Beyond The Designs

In Part III, we will look beyond the designs that enhance learning. In a constructive learning environment, instructors are learners as well. This part should suggest some ideas to improve online collaborative learning community teaching. In an effective online collaborative learning community, learners should be responsible to assist the instructor in improving their teaching. This part focuses on the ideas in improving teaching skills.

CHAPTER 11

Collaborative Evaluation of Teaching

A major institutional consideration to improve teaching, and to determine the timing of promotion, is the evaluation of faculty teaching performance. The common techniques used in evaluating teaching are peer evaluations and student evaluations. The criteria used for face-to-face teaching may not be appropriate for evaluating online teaching because online teaching frequently avoids lectures. Therefore, the question that occurs is how we should evaluate online teaching. When applied to online teaching, these methods are plagued by inconsistent results because the aspects evaluated in online teaching and online learning differs from face-to-face teaching. This chapter introduces a formative and descriptive evaluation that integrates both peer evaluation of teaching and student evaluation of teaching to improve the evaluation of the online collaborative learning community.

This approach to evaluation may appear not to fit the concept of an online collaborative learning community; however, if we examine the collaborative learning community closely, we realize that the instructors are also learners. Therefore, it is important to improve the teaching skills of the instructor in the online collaborative learning community by integrating the instructor into the community of learners and peers. This evaluation concept is beyond the classroom collaboration. Improving instructors' teaching skills through evaluating their teachings is critical.

This online teaching evaluation consists of three stages: a preliminary communication, ongoing evaluations and discussions, and feedback and debriefing.

DESIGN 19 PRELIMINARY COMMUNICATION

Specifics

What	Entire class
Who	Learners, instructors, peer instructors
When	First week of the class
How	Invite guest moderators
Technology	E-mail, listserv, threaded discussion, real-time chat, audio/video conferencing systems
Duration	1 week
Grade	

In the preliminary stage, there are three roles to be established to initiate the evaluation process. They are the Peer Evaluation Committee, peer evaluators, and instructors.

Task 1: Form a Peer Evaluation Committee

First, a Peer Evaluation Committee should be formed to assume the responsibility of establishing policy and procedures of peer evaluation, and implementation of the peer evaluation. The committee can be composed of instructors, instructional designers, organization administrators, human resources staff, etc.

Task 2: Identify Peer Evaluations

The second role to be identified is the peer evaluator whose responsibilities are to conduct and facilitate actual evaluation of teaching. In the larger teaching department, it may be necessary to form a pool of peer evaluators, permitting the committee to assign any one from the pool to evaluate any particular teaching. Peer evaluators can be selected from among the senior instructors (who have more teaching experience), instructor mentors (who assist and guide junior instructors), and other instructors.

Regardless of how selection occurs, the peer evaluator must possess a few critical skills. The peer evaluator (a) has online teaching experience; (b) is familiar with online discussion moderations, and (c) holds similar content expertise as the instructor.

Task 3: Prepare Evaluating Criteria

The third role is the instructor. Ideally, all instructors should be evaluated by their teaching and teaching performances regardless of the amount of teaching experience they have.

Task 4: Meet with the Instructor

The next step begins with a meeting of the instructor with the peer evaluator. In this meeting, the peer evaluator should explain the process and the purpose of the integrated teaching evaluation to ensure that the instructor understands the evaluation process. The peer evaluator should also present a set of discussion questions that will be used in discussions between the peer evaluator and the students later in the teaching session. These questions are:

1. What about the instructional practices of this instructor worked to enhance your learning and development during this course?
2. What about this instructor's practices hindered or detracted from your learning and development?
3. If we could go back to the beginning of the course and start over, what specific things would you suggest that the instructor do to improve your learning experience?

The instructor, therefore, is informed on how he or she will be evaluated; most importantly, the instructor must understand that the evaluation is based on his or her statement of their teaching philosophy. During this first meeting, if the instructor is unclear about the evaluation process, questions can be resolved before the evaluation proceeds.

Task 5: Post Teaching Philosophy

At the beginning of the online teaching, the instructor should post his/her teaching philosophy online and address the design of the online instruction, effective ways to learn, and what is expected of students. This process allows the instructor to determine a set of evaluation criteria. The instructor posts this information online as a part of the teaching instruction and in the course syllabus. Haugen (1998) recommended several guidelines for writing a sound statement of teaching philosophy:

1. Describe what your students are to learn from the fundamental content of the courses you teach.

2. Explain whether your hope is to foster critical thinking, facilitate acquiring life-long learning skills, and prepare students to work effectively in an information economy, or develop problem-solving strategies.

3. Define your role in orienting students to a discipline, and what it means to be an educated person in your field. Explain how you delineate your areas of responsibility compared to your students' responsibilities.

4. Clarify the specific ways in which you want to improve the education of students in your field.

5. Refer to discussions in academic journals or in professional organizations about shortcomings in the education of students today or unmet needs in the discipline. Explain your ideas about how to address those shortcomings and needs.

Task 6: Inform Learners

The peer evaluator informs the students by e-mail, announcement, or other electronic forms about the evaluation of online teaching and invites the assistance of the students to participate in this process. Students are required to read and review the teaching philosophy statement and to use it as a tool in the evaluation process later in the teaching. Adult learning principles reveal that adults are self-motivated. Therefore, learners are able to recognize the value of participating in the evaluation as a major incentive to reach their learning goals. Reading the teaching philosophy will assist students to be more capable to work with the instructor and permit the instructor to assist the students in attaining their personal learning goals. The purpose of this process is to inform the students of the online teaching evaluation process; therefore, the students will consider the online teaching and their learning experiences.

DESIGN 20 ONLINE EVALUATION AND DISCUSSIONS

Specifics

What	Discuss and evaluate the instructor's online instruction design and teaching skills.
Who	Learners, instructors, peer instructors
When	Before the learners' grades are assigned
How	Recruit volunteer learners; conduct collaborative evaluations; summarize the evaluations
Technology	Threaded discussion or real-time chat
Duration	1–2 weeks (threaded discussion); 1 hour at least (real-time discussion)
Grade	There is no need to assign points for this activity since it is volunteer work.

The second stage, later in the teaching session, discussions of online teaching evaluation will occur that require the participation of the peer evaluator and the students. The instructor should be excluded from this evaluation process.

Task 1: Recruit the Students

The peer evaluator communicates with the students by e-mail , or other communication forms, announcing the online discussion to evaluate online teaching, and invites their assistance to take part in this process. Students should be informed that all personal information will be confidential, and only general comments will be provided to the instructor in the formal report. The students who agree to participate in this evaluation discussion will be given access to a password-protected site to participate in the discussions. For reasons of privacy and confidentiality, passwords are given only to the peer evaluator and the students who wish to participate. Students who agree to take part in this evaluation discussion should receive an e-mail from the peer evaluator informing them of the discussion Web site, log on information, and the questions to be discussed before the discussions begin, allowing the students more time to address the discussion questions. Being prepared allows the students to contribute substantial comments to this evaluation process.

Task 2: Evaluation Discussion

An online discussion space should be created to allow the peer evaluator and the students to conduct evaluation discussions. This online discussion space can be designed with either asynchronous (threaded discussions) or synchronous (real-time chat) discussion forms. If a threaded discussion format is adopted for the evaluation, ample time should be allowed for completion since asynchronous communication is a more time-consuming process. A minimum of one hour in a week should be devoted to the process to ensure that all the discussion questions are addressed if real-time chat is the discussion format. Generally, the real-time discussions should be scheduled with considerations of the students' free time since most of students have a full-time work commitment. Therefore, scheduling should be done carefully with considerations for all students.

Regardless of which discussion format is selected, the students should begin by responding to the three discussion questions posted by the evaluator. Once everyone has shared their responses to these questions, the participants of the discussion can append comments and reflections to each other's postings. The peer evaluator must ensure that all participants reach a consensus on each of the discussion questions. The peer evaluator can request that all participating students post their responses to the first of the three discussion questions if the format is asynchronous. When the responses to the first question have been posted, the students can respond to comments made by their fellow students. The peer evaluator should move to the next discussion question when a consensus is reached. Discussion on all the questions can begin simultaneously when the format is asynchronous; also, it is important that students respond to all three discussion questions before commenting on the responses of their fellow correspondents.

The evaluation discussions should be completed before the teaching session is finished. The validity of the evaluation may be compromised if the discussion has not been completed before the grades are posted. This bias should be avoided. The discussion space should be password protected to assure privacy and confidentiality, allowing access only to the peer evaluator and the students who agree to participate.

The peer evaluator facilitates the evaluation discussions by functioning as a moderator and encourages responses to the evaluation questions. Participants are required to use their real name during the discussions rather than participating anonymously because the students must be responsible for their comments. Students should be informed that the purpose of the evaluation discussions is to assist the instructor to improve his or her instructional designs and the teaching skills; behaviors that include flaming and personal attacks are to be avoided.

Online moderation skills are critical in the evaluation discussion process. Tu and Corry (2003) recommend several useful guidelines to facilitate online discussion. They are:

1. Facilitating regularly: Monitor the discussions as often as possible during the time you are moderating.
2. Encouraging: Make sure that all students join in regularly in the discussions and publicly recognize them. If you find that someone is not participating, it is appropriate to e-mail the person individually with a warm message and invite him or her to become an active discussion participant.
3. Evolving: If certain questions have been well discussed, the evaluator should post new questions or advance the discussion to a different level.
4. Dialogue: Be clear, concise, and conversational. Create a more social and a more pragmatic dialogue.
5. Clarifying: Clarify the messages if the postings are not clear to the participants.
6. Tone: Ensure that participants feel welcome and safe, and model the use of the virtual medium to minimize miscommunication.
7. Support: Be encouraging, supportive, timely, and constructive in all discussions and all evaluations of the results of the discussions.

Task 3: Summarize the Discussions

The peer evaluator should summarize the discussions and review them with the students after the discussion period is completed. This summary forms the essence of the formal report given to the instructor. The names of the students are not included in the summary. Issues to be addressed by the instructor raised during the discussion are appropriately included in the summary. The completed summary should be shared with the participating students and should be updated if more comments are generated. Throughout the process, the peer evaluator is involved in collecting and synthesizing the information.

DESIGN 21 FEEDBACK AND DEBRIEFING

Specifics

What	Provide feedback to the instructor
Who	Learners, instructors, peer instructors
When	Last week of the class or later in the class
How	Provide the instructor feedback; address issues; report back the volunteer learner group; file the final report
Technology	E-mail
Duration	3–4 days
Grade	No grade is assigned.

Task 1: Present Evaluation

The peer evaluator presents the summary to the instructor after it is finished. The instructor should peruse the summary with the peer evaluator, who should advise the subject of any issues to be addressed.

Task 2: Question Evaluation

Questions raised by the instructor should be clarified and explained by the peer evaluator. The instructor's responses to the summary are to be forwarded to the students who participated in the evaluation process.

Task 3: File the Evaluation

After the instructor agrees with the summary, this summary will serve as a final evaluation of online teaching and it can be filed in the instructor's personnel dossier.

REMINDERS

The formative and descriptive integration of peer evaluation of teaching and student evaluation of teaching is an effective way to improve the design of online instruction and the teaching skills of online instructors.

One should not assume that one evaluation is more effective than others (Seldin, 1993). In fact, different types of teaching evaluations can be applied, such as a teaching portfolio, to evaluate teaching quality.

Selecting a peer evaluator is a critical process. The qualifications of peer evaluators are important because of the significant role they play in the evaluation process. They must include skill as a facilitator. This may require instruction for peer evaluators on how to conduct the evaluations. This evaluation focuses on integrating the values of formative and descriptive evaluations; therefore, it takes longer to accomplish. It may not be appropriate for short-term teaching courses or sessions.

REFLECTIONS

Evaluation of teaching is an important process in online teaching and learning. Traditionally, the peer evaluation of teaching (PET) and the student evaluation of teaching (SET) correlate weakly because of a lack of understanding of the instructor's teaching belief and philosophy. Integrating PET and SET in a formative evaluation reduces the conflict between these two types of evaluations. The results of teaching evaluation from formative and descriptive integration processes provide better value to the students, the peer evaluators, the instructor, and the administrators.

CHAPTER 12

Finis

There is no perfect instruction design. Online collaborative learning community (OCLC) has its own weaknesses although it has many advantages to enhance online learning. Ill-structured small-group instruction may result in resentment among learners regarding the fairness of grading systems, lack of support, the feeling of unequal distribution of labor, and other issues. It is important to be aware of the potential negative impacts and limitations of designs projected in this book so that readers may have a better understanding on both strengths and weaknesses of OCLC. Some of these potential challenges arise naturally while considering the following can prevent others.

SLOW SOCIAL CHANGE

Online learning does not work as efficiently as traditional face-to-face learning. Generally, it takes longer for learners to achieve consensus on team communication decisions. Therefore, there is risk that a team may not be able to complete the required tasks. It is also important to know that social change is a slow process, even in a traditional face-to-face environment. Unfortunately, in regular academic systems, a course may last about fifteen weeks or even less. It is challenging to develop a collegial social relationship between and among learners within such a limited period of time. For that reason, the instructor must actively support the social process of the teams to improve and increase the online social presence of learners and instructors.

Due to the longer process of the OCLC, the instructor is required to monitor and facilitate collaborative activities intensively and closely. It demands more time and effort by the instructor to ensure that all teams are making progress throughout the entire course of the class. It is important to supply adequate attention and support to each individual team. Dedicating learning responsibilities does not mean freeing the instructor of teaching responsibilities. Enthusiasm, dedication, time, and patience emerge as keys to the success of OCLC.

APPRECIATION OF VALUES

Collaborative learning may not be new to most learners; however, their experiences, reaction, appreciation, and expectations are widely varied. The main purpose of collaborative learning is to engage learners in a rich critical thinking process, an information exchanging process, a knowledge generating process, and reaching rich and interactive learning experiences. If learners do not fully understand the purposes of collaborative learning and appreciate the value of collaborative learning, they will focus on achievement/grades only and they would not engage in collaborative activities effectively. It is important to advise learners about reasonable and logical expectations for the OCLC.

When learners have misunderstood OCLC, it is not uncommon that OCLC designs fail and teams fall apart. Due to the lack of visual communication, weekly face-to-face communication, and focusing on the end-products only, rather than valuing end-products and processes, online learners can lose track very easily and emerge with different goals. If learners do not report their difficulties or communicate effectively with the instructor, the instructor will be ignorant of team progress because of the absence of various social context cues, such as facial expressions, body language, speaking tones, etc. Teams and learners may feel frustrated and lack motivation to continue team activities. The result is teams fall apart, run off track, and fail to finish team tasks.

ACCOUNTABILITY OF ASSESSMENT

Peer evaluations and self-evaluations may not be trustworthy. Frequently, social relationships have a great deal of influence on the peer evaluation. Ideally, the collaborative evaluations may address and balance the weakness of self and peer evaluations. To increase the accountability of assessment, effective peer and self-evaluation methods and instructions must be presented to assist students in conducting evaluations.

APPROPRIATE USE OF TECHNOLOGIES

The availability and uses of technologies does not necessarily guarantee the success with implementation of an OCLC. Frequently, it is heard "I used all kinds of technologies to support my online students. Unfortunately, the technologies failed on me." The phenomenon arises from inappropriate selection and use of technologies. Simply placing technologies into an online class does not result in effective use of technologies. The issue depends on the appropriate selection and use of technologies. In other words, the point is how well we put them together, not what we have.

FEAR OF SUFFICIENT CONTENT COVERAGE

Naturally, the instructor may fear that all of materials in a course may not be able to be covered via the instructional design of an OCLC. This issue lies in how well the framework, implementation, support, and assessment have been deliberated. A healthy OCLC should improve learning in both width and depth. It is the instructor's responsibility to monitor and improve their OCLC designs constantly. In other words, dedicated instructors for OCLC should be familiar with OCLC planning, organization, management, and implementation, in addition to being willing to challenging themselves to advance their teaching proficiencies.

REFLECTIONS

The foundation of an effective interactive OCLC is communication. Communication is learning. Instructors should frequently dedicate themselves to communicating with their students to motivate and assist learners to initiate, sustain, and complete their online learning throughout the course. The instructor must communicate regularly, via e-mail or other computer-mediated communication forms, with every team and each individual throughout the course to provide support and monitor progress. Providing frequent feedback allowing students to modify their learning strategies is critical, such as a mid-semester team report can be integrated to supply information that may be missed by simple observation. Additionally, instructors must attend discussions and team communications to provide psychological and substantive support. This process provides the instructor with information about the progress of the teams and permits early corrective intervention. Active participation may not be necessary; a simple demonstration of social presence by the instructor may be adequate. In this manner, instructors individualize guidance and lead students to achieve their learning goals.

Appendix: A Collaborative Evaluation Form

	Instructor	Self-Evaluation	Peer Evaluation 1	Peer Evaluation 2	Peer Evaluation 3	Total
Your Name						
Team Members						
Point Allocation	50%	Fill in	Fill in	Fill in	Fill in (if applic-able)	100%

* The point allocation should be based on discussion and agreement by your team.

Self-Evaluation	
Points	
Notes	Provide an explanation for the instructor.

Peer Evaluation 1	
Name	
Point	
Feedback	Provide feedback for your teammate.

Peer Evaluation 2	
Name	
Point	
Feedback	Provide feedback for your teammate.

Peer Evaluation 3	
Name	
Point	
Feedback	Provide feedback for your teammate.

Resources

ONLINE COLLABORATIVE LEARNING

The Center for Collaborative Learning & Communication, Furman University—http://alpha.furman.edu/~jlove/cclc/

Collaborative E-Learning in Higher Education—http://www.shef.ac.uk/collaborate/collaborative_elearning/collaborative_e-learning.shtml

Collaborative Learning, University of Maryland University College—http://www.umuc.edu/virtualteaching/module1/collaborative.html

Collaborative Learning, University of Minnesota—http://dmc.umn.edu/strategies/collaborative.shtml

Online Collaborative Learning in Higher Education—http://clp.cqu.edu.au/

ONLINE DEBATE

About Debating and How to Start, Australian Capital Territory Debating Union—http://www.actdu.org.au/archives/actein_site/aboutd.html

Debate, Annette Lamb and Larry Johnson—http://www.42explore.com/debate.htm

Debate Central—http://debate.uvm.edu/

Debate Comics—http://www.debatecomics.org/the_white_rose.asp

Designing Online Debate—http://onlinelearn.edschool.virginia.edu/debate/

DebateUSA.com—http://debateusa.com/

A Guide to Parliamentary Debate, American Parliamentary Debate Association—http://www.apdaweb.org/guide/

Introduction to the Way of Reason, Alfred C. Snider, University of Vermont—http://debate.uvm.edu/code/001.html

John R. Prager's Debate Site—http://pws.chartermi.net/~johnprager/

On Debating—http://www.truthtree.com/debates.shtml

Public Debate—http://www.publicdebate.com.au/reaction/

Speech Activity Links, the Michigan Interscholastic Forensic Association—http://www.themifa.org/links.html

YouDebate.Com—http://www.youdebate.com/

ONLINE MODERATIONS

Developing learning through effective online moderation—http://www.ilt.ac.uk/downloads/031027_AL_Salmon.pdf

Effective Online Facilitation—http://www.flexiblelearning.net.au/guides/facilitation.html

EModerators, Berge Collins Associates—http://www.emoderators.com/moderators.shtml

Forum Moderating, University of Minnesota—http://ltu.cce.umn.edu/guide/design_dev/moderator.html

Guidelines for Moderating Online Educational Computer Conferences, David Winograd—http://www.emoderators.com/moderators/winograd.html

Moderating Online Chat Rooms—http://ai-depot.com/Essay/Moderation.html

Online Focus Group Moderating Tips, Lynda Maddox—http://www.iresearch.com/pages/library/focus_guidelines.cfm

Online Moderation—http://www.acr.net.au/marg99/Research/

OnlineFacilitation.com, Full Circle Associates—http://www.onlinefacilitation.com/

Resources for Moderators, Education Network of Ontario—http://www.enoreo.on.ca/resources/moderator_res.htm

Virtual Games for Real Learning: Fast, Cheap, Effective, the NET*Working 2000—http://flexiblelearning.net.au/nw2000/talkback/p51.htm

COMMUNITY OF PRACTICE (CoP)

Building Online Professional Networks: Three Stages to Success, Suzanne Rainey—http://www.onlinecommunityreport.com/features/rainey

Communities of Practice, Community Intelligence Labs—http://www.co-i-l.com/coil/knowledge-garden/cop/index.shtml

Community of Practice (CoP) Definitions—http://www.kmadvantage.com/cop.htm

CoPs (Communities of Practice), TCM.COM—http://www.tcm.com/trdev/cops.htm

USAID Community of Practice Simulation—http://knowledge.usaid.gov/copgame.html

References

Baum, D., & Baum, C. (1986). Learners, know thyself: Self-assessment and self-determined assessment in education. *The New Era, 67*(3), 65–67.

Baynton, M. (1992). Dimensions of "control" in distance education: A factor analysis. *The American Journal of Distance Education, 6*(2), 17–31.

Berge, Z. L., & Muilenburg, L. (2000). Designing discussion questions for online adult learning. *Educational Technology, 40*(5), 53–56.

Boud, D. J. (1986). *Implementing student self assessment.* Sydney, Australasia: Higher Education Research and Development Society of Australasia.

Brooks, D. W. (1997). *Web-teaching: A guide to designing interactive teaching for the World Wide Web.* New York: Plenum Press.

Bruffee, K. A. (1995). Sharing our toys. *Change, 27*(1), 12–18.

Bulman, T. (1996). *Peer assessment in group work.* Retrieved July 12, 2002 from http://www.oaa.pdx.edu/CAE/FacultyFocus/spring96/bulman.html.

Burns, C. W. (1998). Peer evaluation of teaching: Claims vs. research. (ERIC Reproduction Service No. ED421470).

Bush, V. (1945). As we may think. *The Atlantic Monthly, 176*(1), 101–108.

Cavanagh, R. R. (1996). Formative and summative evaluation in the faculty peer review of teaching. *Innovative Higher Education, 20*(4), 235–240.

Centra, J. A. (1987). Formative and summative evaluation: Parody or paradox? Techniques for evaluating and improving instruction. In L. M. Aleamoni (Ed.), *New Directions for Teaching and Learning No. 31* (pp.47–55). San Francisco: Jossey-Bass.

Centra, J. A. (1993). *Reflective faculty evaluation: Enhancing teaching and determining faculty effectiveness.* San Francisco, CA: Jossey-Bass.

Collaborative Visualization (CoVis) Project. (2000). *Communities of practice.* Retrieved July 11, 2000 from http://www.covis.nwu.edu/info/philosophy/communities-of-practice.html.

Cooper, J., & Robinson, P. (1998). Small group instruction in science, mathematics, engineering, and technology: A discipline status report and a teaching agenda for the future. *Journal of College Science Teaching, 27*(6), 383–388.

Cummings, L. L., & Bromiley, P. (1996). The organizational trust inventory (OTI): Development and validation. In R. M. Kramer & T. R. Tyler (Eds.), *Trust in organizations: Frontiers of theory and research* (pp. 302–330). Thousand Oaks, CA: Sage Publications.

Dickstein, R., & McBride, K. B. (1998). Listserv lemmings and fly-brarians on the wall: A librarian-instructor team taming the cyberbeast in the large classroom. *College & Research Libraries, 59*(1), 10–17.

Eisenstadt, M. (1995). *The knowledge media generation.* Retrieved September 11, 2001 from http://kmi.open.ac.uk/kmi-misc/kmi-feature.html.

Engel, C., & Schaeffer, E. (2001). Learning to persuade and persuading to learn: Design and evaluation of an online debate forum for large lecture classes. Paper presented at the European CSCL Conference.

Falchikov, N. (1993). Group process analysis: Self and peer assessment of working together in a group. *Educational and Training Technology International, 30*(3), 275–284.

Falchikov, N. (1995). Peer feedback making: Developing peer assessment. *Innovations in Education and Training International, 32*(2), 175–187.

Falchikov, N. (1986). Product comparisons and process benefits of collaborative peer group and self assessments. *Assessment and Evaluation in Higher Education, 11*(2), 146–166.

Garrison, D. R. (1993). Quality and access in distance education. In D. Keegan (Ed.), *Theoretical principles of distance education* (pp. 9–21). New York: Routledge.

Gerdy, K. B. (1998). If Socrates only knew: Expanding law class discourse. Paper presented at the Annual Conference for Law Schools Computing. Chicago, IL.

Gilbert, S. W. (2002). Connectedness and self-revelation. *Syllabus, 16*(4), 23, 36.

Golub, J. (1988). *Focus on collaborative learning.* Urbana, IL: National Council of Teachers of English.

Gould, C. (1991). Converting faculty assessment into faculty development: The director of composition's responsibility to probationary faculty. (ERIC Document Reproduction Service ED331068).

Graham, G. (1997). Community, virtual community and community networks: The telecommunities Canada position on "Public Lanes," universal access and electronic public space. *Paper presented at Universal Access Workshop, Information Policy Research Program.*

Gunawardena, C. N. (1995). Interaction—Affirmative. (Opening Statement). ICDE95: Debate on Interaction. Retrieved March 15, 1999 from http://www.ualberta.ca/~tanderso/icde95/interaction_www/0009.html

Gunawardena, C. N., & McIsaac, M. S. (2003). Distance education. In D. Jonassen (Ed.), *Handbook for research on educational communications and technology* (pp. 355–396). New York: Simon and Schuster.

Haugen, L. (1998). *Writing a teaching philosophy statement.* Retrieved March 3, 2003 from http://www.cte.iastate.edu/tips/philosophy.html.

Honebein, P. (1996). Seven goals for the design of constructivist learning environments. In B. G. Wilson (Ed.), *Constructivist learning environments: Case studies in instructional design* (pp. 11–24). Englewood Cliffs, NJ: Educational Technology Publications.

Horgan, D. (1991). Peer review: It works. Paper presented at Annual Meeting of American Educational Research Association.

Hutchings, P. (1996). The peer review of teaching: Progress, issues and prospects. *Innovative Higher Education, 20*(4), 221–234.

Jarvenpaa, S. L., Knoll, K., & Leidner, D. E. (1998). Is anybody out there? Antecedents of trust in global virtual teams. *Journal of Management Information Systems, 14*(4), 29–64.

Keegan, D. (1993). Reintegration of the teaching acts. In D. Keegan (Ed.), *Theoretical principles of distance education* (pp. 113–134). New York: Toutledge.

Keig, L. W., & Waggoner, M. D. (1994). Collaborative peer review: The role of faculty in improving college teaching. *ASHE-ERIC Higher Education Report No. 2.* (ERIC Reproduction Service No. ED378925).

Keig, L. W., & Waggoner, M. D. (1995). Peer review of teaching: Improving college instruction through formative assessment. *Journal on Excellence in College Teaching, 6*(3), 51–83.

Kramer, R. M., & Tyler, T. R. (1996). *Trust in organizations: Frontiers of theory and research*. Thousand Oaks, CA: Sage.

Latham, G. P., & Locke, E. A. (1991). Self-regulation through goal setting. *Organizational Behavior and Human Decision Processes, 20*, 212–247.

Lieberman, A. (1996). Creating intentional learning communities. *Educational Leadership, 54*(3), 51–55.

Marsh, H. W. (1987). Students' evaluations of university teaching: Research findings, methodological issues, and directions for future research. *International Journal of Educational Research, 17*, 253–388.

Mayer, R. C., Davis, J. H., & Schoorman, F. D. (1995). An integrative model of organizational trust. *Academy of Management Review, 20*(3), 709–734.

McAllister, D. J. (1995). Affect- and cognition-based trust as foundations for interpersonal cooperation in organizations. *Academy of Management Journal, 38*(1), 24–59.

McDermott, R. (2000). *Knowing in community: 10 critical success factors in building communities of practice*. Retrieved July 11, 2000 from http://www.co-i-l.com/coil/knowledge-garden/cop/knowing.shtml.

McDermott, R. (1998). Knowing is a human act: How information technology inspired but cannot deliver knowledge management. *California Management Review, Summer*.

McMaster, M. (1999). *Communities of practice: An introduction*, Retrieved July 11, 2000 from http://www.co-i-l.com/coil/knowledge-garden/cop/mmintro.shtml

Morrison, T. R. (1995). Global transformation and the search for a new educational design. *International Journal of Lifelong Education, 14*(3), 188–213.

National Science Foundation. (1997). The challenge and promise of K-8 science education reform. National Science Foundation: A monograph for professionals in science, mathematics, and technology education, volume 1. Washington, DC: National Science Foundation.

Norton, R. W. (1986). Communicator style in teaching: Giving good form to content. In J. M. Civikly (Ed.), *Communicating in college classrooms* (pp. 33–40). San Francisco, CA: Jossey-Bass Inc.

Ocker, R. J., & Yaverbaum, G. (1999). Asynchronous computer-mediated communication versus face-to-face collaboration: Results on student learning, quality and satisfaction. *Group Decision and Negotiation, 8,* 427–440.

Osborne, J. L. (1998). Integrating student and peer evaluation teaching. *College Teaching, 46*(1), 36–38.

Panitz, T. (1996). A definition of collaborative vs. cooperative learning. Retrieved March 18, 2002 from http://www.lgu.ac.uk/deliberations/collab.learning/panitz2.html.

Peter+Trudy Johnson-Lenz, A. T. (2000). Community of practice. Retrieved July 29, 2000 from http://www.awaken.com/at/Awaken.nsf?OpenDatabase.

Renyi, J. (1996). *Teachers Take Charge of Their Learning: Transforming Professional Development for Student Success,* Retrieved July 29, 2000 from http://www.nfie.org/takechar.htm

Rowntree, D. (1987). *Assessing students: how shall we know them?* London: K. Page.

Roschelle, J., Penuel, W. R., & Abrahamson, L. (2004). The networked classroom. Paper presented at the Annual Conference of American Educational Research Association (AERA). April 12–16, 2004. San Diego, CA.

Schaeffer, E. L., McGrady, J. A., Bhargava, T., & Engel, C. (2002). Online debate to encourage peer interactions in the large lecture setting: Coding and analysis of forum activity. Paper presented at Annual Meeting of American Educational Research Association.

Schlager, M., Fusco, J., & Schank, P. (2000). Evolution of an on-line education community of practice. Paper presented at the Annual Conference of American Educational Research Association.

Scott, M. B., & Lyman, S. M. (1968). Accounts. *American Sociology Review, 33*(1), 46–62.

Seldin, P. (1993). *Successful use of teaching portfolios.* Bolton, MA: Anker.

Sharp, J. (1997). *Key hypotheses in supporting communities of practice.* Retrieved July 11, 2000 from http://www.tfriend.com/hypothesis.html.

Sluijsmans, D., Dochy, F., & Moerkerke, G. (1999). Creating a learning environment by using self-, peer-, and co-assessment. *Learning Environments Research, 1*(3), 293–319.

Snow, C. C., Snell, S. A., & Davison, S. C. (1996). Use transnational teams to globalize your company. *Organizational Dynamics, 24*(4), 50–67.

Somervell, H. (1993). Issues in assessment, enterprise and higher education: The case for self-, peer and collaborative assessment. *Assessment and Evaluation in Higher Education, 18*(3), 221–233.

Stokes, L., Sato, N., McLaughlin, M., & Talbert, J. (1997). *Theory-based reforms and the problem of change: Contexts that matter for teacher's learning and community.* Stanford, CA: Stanford University, Center for Research on the Context of Teaching.

Tu, C. H. (2003). Building an online collaborative learning community. In M. Silberman (Ed.), *The 2003 training and performance sourcebook and the 2002 team and organization development sourcebook* (pp. 303–312). Wappingers Falls, NY: Inkwell Publishing.

Tu, C. H. (2000). Critical examination of factors affecting interaction on CMC. *Journal of Network and Computer Applications, 23*(1), 39–58.

Tu, C. H. (1999). Do we know how to speak online? *Society for Information Technology and Teacher Education International Conference.* Norfolk, VA: Association for the Advancement of Computing in Education (AACE) .

Tu, C. H. (2004). Electronic community of practice. In M. Silberman (Ed.), *The 2004 training and performance sourcebook and the 2004 team and organization development sourcebook.* Wappingers Falls, NY: Inkwell Publishing.

Tu, C. H. (2002). The impacts of text-based computer-mediated communication on online social presence. *Journal of Interactive Online Learning, 1*(2).

Tu, C. H., & Corry, M. (2003). Designs, managements, and strategies in asynchronous learning discussions. *The Quarterly Review of Distance Education, 4*(3), 303–315.

Tu, C. H., & Corry, M. (2002). E-learning community. *The Quarterly Review of Distance Education, 3*(3), 207–218.

Tu, C. H., & McIsaac, M. S. (2001). Community of practice for mentoring. Paper presented at the Annual Conference of American Educational Research Association (AERA).

Tu, C. H., & McIsaac, M. S. (2002). An examination of social presence to increase interaction in online classes. *The American Journal of Distance Education, 16*(3), 131–150.

Tu, C. H., Yen, C. J., Corry, M., & Ianacone, R. (2003). Integrating peer evaluation of teaching and student evaluation for online instruction. *Society for Information Technology and Teacher Education International Conference.* Norfolk, VA: Association for the Advancement of Computing in Education (AACE).

Walther, J. B., & Burgoon, J. K. (1992). Relational communication in computer-mediated interaction. *Human Communication Research, 19*, 50–88.

Weiser, M., & Morrison, J. (1998). Project memory: Information management for project team. *Journal of Management Information System, 14*(3), 149–166.

Index

assessment, 7, 11, 15, 21, 23–28, 40, 42, 62, 63, 75, 107, 108, 109, 111, 126, 127; collaborative evaluation, 7, 8, 23, 24, 35, 37, 107–124, 126; evaluations of teaching, 26, 27; peer evaluation, 8, 23–27, 36–37, 39–40, 45, 107–111, 113, 117–118, 123–124, 126; self evaluation, 23–26, 37, 108–111, 113, 126
assignments, 7, 25, 36, 37, 38, 39–46

collaboration, 3, 4, 5, 7, 8, 11–27, 31, 34, 35, 37, 39, 40, 41, 43, 45, 47, 49, 51, 53, 55, 57, 59, 61, 63, 85, 89, 90, 94, 96, 109, 112, 117
communication strategies, 99, 102, 103
Computer-Mediated Communication (CMC), 4, 17, 19, 20, 31, 44, 53, 54, 56, 67, 73, 77, 82, 94, 95, 97, 98, 101, 102, 103, 110, 127; communication channels, 5, 20, 83, 95; e-mail, 19, 35, 37, 39, 41, 42, 50, 51, 52, 65, 67, 68, 69, 71, 74, 77, 78, 79, 81, 85, 86–96, 98, 102, 104, 107, 110, 118, 120, 121, 122, 123, 127; emoticons and paralanguages, 96, 103; keyboarding, 88, 95, 101; Listserv, 19, 74, 78–79, 85–87, 89, 93–95, 118; stylistic

communication strategies, 102; threaded discussion board, 5, 19, 33, 35, 39, 42, 43, 44, 47, 49, 52, 65, 68, 71, 77, 81, 85–88, 92–95, 98, 102, 104, 105, 112, 113
cooperation, 11, 12, 111

debate, 7, 8, 14, 47, 52–63, 76, 113

knowledge management, 11, 18–21, 69, 78, 79, 85

learning community, 30; Community of Practice (CoP), 7, 17, 18, 73–83; e-Learning community, 17, 18; guest moderators, 7, 18, 65, 70, 71; guest speakers, 70; social context, 6, 18, 95, 97, 105; social presence, 44, 62, 72, 125, 127; social relationships, 34, 81, 82, 90, 98, 100, 125, 126; trust, 16, 76, 81–82, 98, 100, 126; virtual experts, 7, 18, 65–71, 113

moderations, 6–8, 34, 36–37, 47–52, 56, 57, 71, 72, 113, 118, 122; collaborative evaluations, 109, 111, 114, 120, 126; guest moderators, 7, 18, 65, 70, 71

online collaborative learning
    community; collaborative
    evaluation. *See* assessment;
    communication technology, 20–21,
    85–86, 88–89; Community of
    Practice (CoP), 7, 17, 18, 73–83;
    debate, 7, 8, 14, 47, 52–63, 76, 113;
    evaluations of teaching, 26, 27; guest
    moderators, 7, 18, 65, 70, 71;
    interactive project presentation, 7,
    14, 39, 43; interactivity, 6, 7, 11–12, 14,
    18, 28, 43, 97, 101, 105; moderations,
    6–8, 34, 36–37, 47–52, 56, 57, 71,
    72, 113, 118, 122; peer support
    assignment. *See* assignments;
    preparation, 31–38; social context,
6, 18, 95, 97, 105; team setting, 34–38;
    virtual experts, 7, 18, 65–71, 113
online collaborative learning
    technology; collaboration technology,
    85–96; technology selection, 94–95

stylistic communication, 102

teaching philosophy, 11, 34, 119–120
technology, 85–96; database-driven
    system, 92, 93; e-agent, 78, 80;
    electronic CoP, 81–82; file
    management systems, 85, 89, 91;
    perceptions, 100; portal, 77, 80,
    85, 89, 90, 93, 93–94; privacy, 77, 98,
    101, 121, 122

About the Author

CHIH-HSIUNG TU, Ph.D., is an assistant professor in Educational Technology at Northern Arizona University, Flagstaff, Arizona. He has published widely in professional journals, addressing both practical and theoretical issues. His extensive experience in teaching online moderated courses provides a rare foundation for his treatment of the subject.